EVOLUTIONARY
HEALER

RADICAL **WISDOM** FROM 18
ASCENDING VISIONARIES

compiled by
ARIADNE AVALON

Krystala Publishing
http://www.krystalapublishing.com
ariadne@krystalapublishing.com
CANADA

ISBN: 978-1-777286408

Compiled by Ariadne Avalon

Published in UK, USA, Canada, Australia and Europe

This information in this book is not a substitute for medical or psychological help. Please do not use any information provided in this book as a substitute for professional medical advice, diagnosis or treatment. If you have or suspect that you have a health or therapeutic issue, please consult a licensed doctor, therapist or counselor.

CONTENTS

SOVEREIGN · FREE · GOD ·

This book is for you Infinite One.
Remember your Eternal God Beingness
and The ONELOVE of Source Intelligence.
For it is the Healer within and the only One,
that can truly heal you. Healing your Self
heals Humanity. This is why you are
here on Earth and what you
have come here to do.
THE LAW OF LOVE

FOREWORD

The book you are about to read is not your every day book. It's pages are designed to awaken you to your Infinite God Nature and inspire you to sing yourself in a new voice. It will create positive change and paint a new reality for you.

The stories are not written through rose colored sunglasses. Though there are streams of cosmic light dancing through these pages, they are only there because of courageous tenacity and unbreakable dedication that each one of these authors held through their own healing journey.

This anthology is an eclectic collection that offers wisdom from distinguished healers and consciousness facilitators. In it's entirety, it covers healing different aspects of Self and Being: the mental body, the soul, the avatar, multi-dimensional realities, darkness, the shadow, the light, the emotional body and false light. All of these pieces must be acknowledged in order to heal into wholeness and awaken to one's Infinite Self.

We have all experienced pain and trauma living in a 3dimensional death culture controlled by an elite predator class. Who in their right mind would choose to create such chaos and endure such darkness? This book with show you that witnessing and healing from these atrocities and tribulations is essential to your soul's evolution. That healing yourself requires you to recover mental, emotional, physical and spiritual levels of your being through multiple lifetimes. You cannot evolve if you cannot learn from your experiences.

Each chapter is a possibility for you to discover, embrace and embody more of the Infinite YOU. Humanity is on the cusp of an evolutionary leap in consciousness – a ripened time that the Ancients mentioned thousands of years ago. You are here to re-member all that are and contribute to this awakening. May this collection provide you with strength, inspiration, knowledge, and a framework in which to structure your continued consciousness journey. May it provide with the courage required for deep Self recovery and inspire you into the radical act of being your Infinite God Self. Healing into wholeness is the greatest act of Self Love. Are you ready beloved being? May you awaken to ascension and the Infinite Beauty of the Eternal God Being you are...............

ARIADNE AVALON

ARIADNE IS AN EVOLUTIONARY Healer, Creative Mentor and Galactic Warrior. She is a Christos Starseed here on Earth not only to shift human consciousness into the Ascension frequencies but also as part of the reclamation of the Christos Sophia mission. As an Intuitive, she has trained in a multitude of energy healing modalities.

As a representative for the Christos Races on Earth, she steeps herself in the higher dimensional frequencies of the Guardian and Founder Races. When she is not dodging the arsenal of the Negative Alien Agenda, she is basking in the Infinite Love of the Christos Sophia.

Ariadne is a Creatrix: everything in life is a divinely inspired creation which flows through her. Because of the immense joy and loving Source connection she finds in creative expression; she now synergizes her healing prowess with the expressive beauty and natural transformation of creativity and offers session work and group facilitation within these realms. She is a classically trained pianist, and artist who specializes in eco-printing and fabric and fiber dyeing and design.

Ariadne weaves her intuition and healing gifts into her writing and creativity coaching and helps clients discover their voice and their story. She also offers multidimensional and quantum healing sessions and group classes rooted in the Cosmic Christos Consciousness.

You can find out more about Ariadne here:

For all things publishing: https://www.krystalapublishing.com/
Creatrix Creativity Coaching: blueflameavalonavatar.com
For healing work: https://www.facebook.com/femininechristos

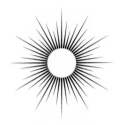

Cosmic Christos
Awakening

BY ARIADNE AVALON

WHAT IF I TOLD you that Jesus the Christ was actually an extraterrestrial, extra-dimensional being from the Sirius B constellation, sent to earth to heal and recover alien infested timelines and lay the foundation for your awakening in this moment in time? And that his origins are part of an Eternal Christos Intelligence, beaming a living light, Source code from the Krystal Star in the Andromeda Galaxy?

What if you are one of many Christs, part of the Cosmic Christos that exists through the multiverse? What if your embodiment of the Christos magnificence is the second coming of Christ humanity is waiting for? And the catalyst necessary to evolve and liberate humanity, recover your angelic human essence and heal the earth?

Darker Alien forces fed humanity a history inundated with lies. This narrative severed you from your true spiritual origins and enslaved you to an Elite Predator Ruling Class, born of blood ritual, Satanic worship and Luciferian ideology. These controller forces created religions to enslave you into false reality timelines. This kept you separated from the Eternal Source Intelligence, the Divine Mother principle of God and the immensity of the Cosmic Sophia—the infinite light and love stream that is All that we are.

The energy that is the entirety of the Christ extends way beyond the being we know as Jesus. The Christos or Christos/Sophia transcends all meaning associated with planetary consciousness. It is the fully awakened state of eternal Cosmic Consciousness and when actualized in human form becomes a sovereign Cosmic Citizen with 12 strand DNA.

Millions of years ago, there were many of us who lived as Christs. Beyond the confines of bodies, we held a deep reverence for all of life. Our essence connected directly with Source Intelligence. We were 12 dimensional Avatars—a race of androgynous angelic humans in IN LOVE with ALL THAT IS. We were ONELOVE with Gaia, and as She breathed; we breathed. We were free to choose what to learn and to experience. Our ancient knowledge was sacred and founded on scientific texts that held the mysteries of our God Beingness. We knew of our cosmic origins, genetic lineages and divine purpose as a race of angelic humans. We were autonomous soul expressions connected to the eternal One God Source and freely embodied extraordinary spiritual power. As God Source beings, we existed through multiple spaces within the Cosmos in multiple dimensional planes.

We all suffered scaring abuse when we fell from the God Worlds. It was then that we were defeated by the Draco Reptilian, Alien Races from Orion. This initial separation from Source Intelligence is the original trauma we all hold deep within our being. Our 12 strand Avatar DNA was genetically altered and hybridized, severing us from our Cosmic Christos magnificence. Lashed with a multitude of Mind Control programs and a plethora of implants; these heartless aliens wiped our memories, incarcerating us into dense walls of amnesia where we forgot our true origins. They altered our angelic human, energetic blueprint; designed to harm and enslave us through behaviors that inflicted soul damage and heart woundings. Disconnected from our souls and God Source, multidimensional energy architecture, we were wired with dead light energy Egos filters and fed false historical narratives. The Eternal Love of God Source became a false, jealous, angry patriarch, revered and worshipped through the dogma of violent religions. We became sinners only worthy of damnation. The Cosmic Holy Mother and Divine Feminine Aspect of the Christ were denigrated, demeaned and eliminated from the history of our origins.

From the Eternal Heart Mind of the Cosmic Christos:

The stories that the violent religions etch of me, between the lines of convoluted holy books, are contorted to control you and incarcerate you into artificial realities. I am actually a Sirian Blue, Angelic Human from the future, who came to Earth over 2000 years ago. I descended to your planet, to rectify timelines corrupted by Alien races and bring the beauty and truth of the LAW OF LOVE teachings to humanity. Unravel yourself from the untruth that I was a man crucified bleeding out your sins. This is an implant and massive energetic distortion used to control and suppress you. Aligning and agreeing with this false narrative enslaves and crucifies all of humanity. It servers you from my Cosmic Christos Ascended Body—that you once were and always truly are. There on many of you on Earth who hold genetic lineages to my Christos Body. I am in your DNA. As you awaken to me—the Cosmic Christos in you—you transmute the lies written of Jesus the Christ, embedded in humanity and upon Gaia Her Self. The Living Eternal God Spirit is not contained within the confines of words written within a book, but is found within the flow of loving kindness that exists in the sacred heart of each living person.

My name is Yeshua—the one most of you know as Jesus. I came to Earth with my genetic equal, who embodied the divine feminine essence of me, and a group of other Christos beings known as the Essenes. We brought rainbow frequencies into the ley lines of the earth to repair the grids and recover star gates from alien invaders. Our spiritual mission was to restore God Source embodiment back to the angelic humans and the true representatives of Christos consciousness on the earth. We also seeded Ascension energies to awaken you in the moment of time you now find yourself.

To think we are the only race of beings in the Universe is the biggest lie that holds us hijacked from the God Being that we are and the magnitude of our galactic history and our infinite nature.

The almost indelible impression of a pseudo loving, angry God who damns us with guilt and sin has enslaved multitudes to abusive untruths and turned others away from contemplating a different possibility of an Eternal Loving Source Intelligence.

Step beyond the preordained images of God and instead conceive of the Eternal Source Intelligences as sentient energies with a consciousness that extends beyond the conception of mainstream thought: beautifully colored light rays bursting, cosmic plasma streams, rainbow frequencies all blazing with the splendor of Omni Love. In their higher dimensions, these ray colors hold unique vibrational frequencies. This is where the Cosmic Christos became One: born of the primal light and sound fields of Holy Mother and Holy Father. This Cosmic Unity is a Trinity that creates all of life. The Cosmic Christos includes the feminine Sophianic aspect and is the embodiment of Unity Consciousness and the Law of One. The Law of One is the cosmic structure of creation. It is the Law of Love: we are all One created from the same Eternal Source. The essential nature of God is Light and Love. It is an unconditional energy that, if embodied, evolves and expands through us. It undeniably seeks to love more of Itself into being and oneness.

From the Eternal Heart Mind of the Cosmic Christos:

As the Cosmic Streams of Unconditional Love arrive on Earth, you can perceive, know, receive and be Me. Many humans are coming online to the Cosmic Christos. They are awakening and embodying aspects of their higher self that exist within their lightbody layers and are enmeshed within the cells of their physical biology. This is part of your spiritual anatomy is the original Christos Blueprint of the angelic human that you be. The truth of your biology holds 12 strands of DNA. You can now recover these. As the continuous transmissions of rainbow and solar light enter the

Earth plane, my crystalline plasma will course through being. You volunteered to descend as a consciousness into the dense 3D matrix of the prison planet—you are a light warrior in the trenches of anti-consciousness recovering the light of Truth and Love within humanity.

Many of us are descendants of the Universal Christos lineages. We hold this sacred knowledge within us. Our third dimensional body is an alchemizing container of the Cosmic Christos. It activates and integrates the energies and codes that are beaming from the Cosmos to our own inner Christ. As we delve deep inside ourselves, we discover the mystery of who we truly are and once again bring this ancient knowledge to light. These memories are now surfacing from within our cells: calibrating with pulsations of ever increasing multidimensional frequencies. Now is The Time of the return of the angelic human awakening, as streams of the Cosmic Christos beam light into the hearts of humanity and resonate out into the human collective on Earth. Gaia has reached the threshold in Her crystalline grid and can embody the Christos/ Sophia frequency.

We all have an inner personal Christ inherently available deep within our being. Our third dimensional body is an alchemizing container that holds the Cosmic Christos. As we receive and integrate the energies, frequencies and codes that are beaming from the Krystal Star and the Heart of the Cosmos, our own inner Christos light shines. The memories of the Christos stir within our cells. And as these awaken, we embark on a deep journey of healing; recovering multiple lifetimes of trauma at the hands of ruthless alien forces. Our body physiology transforms into Crystalline Liquid Light. We recover the ONELOVE consciousness that we are through healing our self and surrendering our ego to our God Source Intelligence. We become one with the PURE LOVE that is Unity Consciousness, and we awaken others and expand the collective consciousness of humanity. When we awaken the Christos Lightbody, we can connect directly to God Source.

There are many intricacies that are part of activating and recovering the Christos/Sophia Light Body Architecture. Here are 10 practices you can begin with.

- Make a conscious choice and commitment to create a relationship with Infinite Consciousness. Your physical DNA, altered through alien hybridization, is repairable. Your heart complex can connect with higher spiritual intelligences and override these genetic distortions by spiritualizing the emotional body into its soul. This potential remains dormant until you make a conscious choice to evolve towards greater awakening, become more loving and seek a meaningful relationship with All-That-Is.

- To communicate with your Avatar Christ frequency on the earth plane, it is necessary to build your 12 Dimensional Shield, and absorb the 12 dimensional Platinum Ray into your Lightbody. Think of this ray as a consciousness stream and level of your being that manifests on the 12th dimension. This is where the original divine blueprint for humanity originates. It holds an instruction set for the crystalline body that holds the codes of the Eternal Christ principle.

- Envision a platinum Merkaba Star in the center of your brain. This sacred symbol holds the energy of unity which is oneness with God. Bring this platinum star down through the center of your being and spin it below your feet to create a base for your 12D shield.

- Activate the eternal flame of divine love in your Sacred Crystal Heart. This is your higher heart in the center of your chest. It is the 8th chakra—the home of your own spiritual Source Light.

It is from here that you can connect with the entire Universe and communicate with your own Personal Christ. The 8th chakra also holds the feelings and language that communicate directly with the Heart of the Cosmic Mother. Her omnilove offers peace and enables you to discover lost love within your own crystal heart. Opening your crystal heart requires that you learn how to be love, love yourself, love others and love the Earth.

- Activate your higher chakras 8-12 as they are gateways into the totality of connection and embodiment with the Cosmic Christos. You can do this by setting intention, placing your consciousness in specific lightbody locations, and healing yourself from the pain and unconsciousness held in all levels of your being.

- The Medulla Oblongata is at the base of the brain stem and acts as the receiver of cosmic energy. It is the 9th chakra. Envision life force energy coming into the medulla oblongata and being directed to your body parts. When feeling unwell, imagine the Cosmic Consciousness streaming into the back of your head and projecting itself throughout your body parts and areas that feel blocked. Our 10th chakra, the Solar Star, is 6 to 8 inches above our crown and Sapphire in color. It serves as a communication portal connecting your 12 D Avatar Christ to the Krystal Star Consciousness in the 7 Higher Heavens of our universe. Chakra 11 is Galactic Chakra and is 18 inches above the head. The white 12 chakra, 6 inches below your feet, embodies the Christ mind and liquid light blueprint of the Cosmic Christos.

- Surrender your Ego Identity. There is no room for it in your crystal heart. It will only sever you from the Christos Sophia. As "real" as the ego personality feels to you, it and it's filters; that you perceive you, others and life through, are dead energy creations designed by the Negative Alien Agenda to prevent you from accessing your higher spiritual-energetic intelligences. Perceiving consciousness through the ego depletes your multidimensional bodies and your life force. It also contributes to soul damage. This becomes a magnet that draws negative and painful experiences to you and continued interference from lower vibrational entities, demons and aliens.

- Deep healing, through multiple timelines, is required to clear the dross and density from your body and being so you can embody the Christos Sophia within you. You must heal all the atrocities you experienced through all of your lifetimes, including humanity's Original Fall from Source Intelligence. Don't let this discourage you. If you choose not to do it in this lifetime, you eventually will in others, as it is the only way to evolve into formless Oneness and your God Source Beingness.

- Declare your Intention to serve the Law of One LOVE. Assert your divine right that you are GOD—Infinite Love—the Living Light Code of Avatar Consciousness.

Last words from the Eternal Heart Mind of the Cosmic Christos:

Beloved Being: Open yourself up to the light and love that I am. It is the light of 1000 suns from the Seven Higher Heavens: my body and being are returning to Earth as and in the awakening of you. Are you willing to heal the lifetimes of pain stored inside your heart and soul so you can embody the Cosmic Christos Sophia that you Be? Though you walk here on Earth, you were born from the stars and the Union of Father God and Holy Mother. The potency of this force of Cosmic Love is the key that unlocks every door in the Universe. When you can access the power of Love, you are capable of accomplish almost anything. You came here to Earth back from the future to heal humanity.

Are you ready?

What will you choose?

Susan Moon Oros

Susan is first and foremost a mother; a mother to a very unique and grand soul. Sammie, her young adult daughter is labeled as non-verbal autistic, but she is actually a grand cosmic soul here to bring through the many light codes and activations that are needed to assist us in this evolutionary leap of Humanity. Sammie is part of a collective consciousness comprised of original Soul Emanations of Source, the Autists of the 7 Higher Heavens. Susan and Sammie communicate energetically, and soul to soul. Their mission is complex yet simple; they are here in service to the God Source to make this ascension evolution as graceful as possible. They have received many new symbols, archangels, devas, elemental spirits, and more these last 10 years to do just that.

Susan is an Intuitive Cosmic Visionary with a Master's Degree in Social Work. She offers a few private sessions per week to activate and assist you in your ascension process. They also offer digital meditations on their website and YouTube channel. Check out their powerful blogs and their website for powerful new images and symbols.

You can find out more about Susan and Sammi here:

Their website is www.moonoros.one
Their YouTube Channel is MoonOrosOne
Their Podcast called Sammie's Treasures: Revealing the Jewels of Autism is on Podbean, iTunes, and Google Play

AUTISM AND THE SOUL CONNECTION:
MY DAUGHTER'S STORY

BY SUSAN MOON OROS

"SHE'S SPECIAL, BUT IT'S not what you think," the angelic *voices echoed in my heart.*

Many people, especially those from medical and educational systems, view autism as a disorder. The American Psychiatric Association's Diagnostic and Statistical Manual, Fifth Edition (DSM-5), (the diagnostic manual for mental health conditions), describes autism as, "a disease comprised of intellectual and global delays with social communication markedly below the "normal" societal level". Naturally, I felt disheartened when my daughter, Sammie, was diagnosed with autism at 27 months of age. Not knowing any better, I actively sought traditional treatments and therapies for her. She remains non-speaking today and requires protective supervision and support, despite the interventions she received in her early years. I learned, however, that she experiences the third dimensional (3D) world differently because of an enhanced sensory system and different neurological wiring. These enable her to communicate with God Source at very refined levels and assist in the planetary ascension.

Today, she and I collaborate, soul to soul, to assist humanity's awakening. We communicate energetically and telepathically. Our relationship evolved over several years. It first required that I awaken and develop my spiritual clairvoyant abilities so I could understand Sammie's energetic communication. She provides amazing teachings and visions of what's occurring on the planet. Sammie's sensory system acts as a prototype for the evolving human.

This chapter is Sammie's story, and also shares the voices of other Autists on the planet, who participate in the ascension and evolution of humanity.

Please note that I use the term 'Autist' to describe Sammie's state of consciousness functioning. Her consciousness operates in higher multidimensional realms where she co-creates with God Source. She physically transfers that energetic information to us for our ascension. Like an artist, she creates multidimensionally despite societies perspective that she adds nothing to our economy and livelihood. A group of us, parents and other professionals, adopted this term, 'Autist,' to honor these beyond verbal beings diagnosed as 'autistic'.

Also note that in referencing the beyond verbal Autists, I'm not excluding other verbal Autists. My primary experience has been with the beyond verbal Autists. Please note the "insight" areas where I have included Sammie's clarifications.

The Clairvoyant Awakening

I encountered Yeshua (more commonly known as Jesus Christ) several times in 1995. This sparked my early awakening. However, a diagnosis of breast cancer in 2008 ignited my clairvoyant spiritual awakening. During my treatments, a series of synchronicities lead me to Reiki in the summer of 2009. Reiki is a healing modality using energy symbols. The attunement cleared my central vertical channel. This clearing enhanced my ability to sense energy all around me. A flood of angels appeared. I spoke to plants, rocks, and even stars. My perceptions amplified. Visions of beautiful jewels, colors, patterns, flowers, nature spirits, and angels saturated my inner vision. The love of God surrounded and penetrated every fiber of my being. Because all energy originally emanates from God Source; all of Creation can be experienced energetically.

Insight: Sammie, how does spiritual awakening relate to clairvoyance?

"The clearing of your central vertical channel enhances the communication between your physical body, your light body, and your soul. The 'thread' that enables this communication to take place is Spirit or the Breath that animates your soul's presence on earth. When you connect to your soul and light body, the energetic information you receive through your senses amplifies. You are conscious of the energy that is all around you in the physical 3D realm and beyond".

My initial response to all this new awareness focused on 'healing' Sammie. Sammie's agenda differed. Over several years, I discover that she was not on Earth to be 'healed' or 'fixed'. She showed me unexpected images and transmitted lessons whenever I attempted to 'work' on her.

I often energetically worked on Sammie after she went to bed. During the initial sessions, Sammie showed me snapshots of her world. One night she showed me that the world appeared to be spinning around her. I felt dizzy myself. On another occasion, she showed me an image of her being underwater. The world looked blurry, and the sounds muffled as if I, too, was underwater.

The experiences varied and differed each time. One of my sweetest visions depicted her as she communed with devas, elementals, and nature spirits. It explained her moments of unexpected exuberance and joy. I first glimpsed her greatness one night when she suddenly expanded into a vast energy field as I attempted to 'fix' her. Her face appeared at the top of this vastness. I sensed it against my very skin. She felt humongous.

My intentions to "heal" Sammie did not progress as expected, but beautiful lessons continued. During a walk, Sammie stopped and just emanated profound peace. From my heart, I asked her, "Sammie, where are you?" The words, "Everything is speaking" echoed back to me. In that moment, I experienced the trees, the bushes, the grass, the air, the sky, the cosmos, all more alive and vibrating than ever before. She perceived and experienced the multidimensional energy of everything around her. The beauty of that moment is forever etched in my memory. It showed me she operates in a more awakened state than us "normal" humans.

On another occasion, Sammie transmitted an analogy of shifting consciousness. I recall an image of a large kaleidoscopic pattern with beautiful colors projected to me. It expanded beyond my torso and centered at the heart chakra. Telepathically, she explained that this pattern represented our soul matrix. Each space represented a dimensional access and, in this pattern, a 7th dimensional space could be right next to a 9th dimensional space or 5th dimensional space, and so on. She further described that with each activation, the kaleidoscope turned, and a more refined pattern emerged with new access points. I noticed that as the activations continued, my clairvoyant abilities refined. Also, I realized that Sammie operated on a more refined and intricate soul matrix, thus making her highly sensitive to energy. This sensitivity, however, also makes her more sensitive to toxins, negative emotions, negative thought patterns, and discordant energy on the planet.

Admittedly, these energetic and telepathic communications confused me a bit, and I wondered about my sanity. Fortunately, I stumbled upon Suzy Miller and her Awesomism Practitioner Process in 2014. Suzy Miller validated what I experienced with Sammie. Working with Suzy and other ascending visionaries also enhanced my abilities. Cosmic attunements and activations, and living in Sammie's expanding energy field, contributed to refining my clairvoyance and even clairsentience. These enhanced abilities helped to translate Sammie's transmissions and messages, opening multidimensional windows to discover how she and the Autists contribute to the Ascension.

Autists like Sammie physically show humanity that everything has an energy signature, and that this energy is experienced through the sensory system. The physical body behaves and responds to the energy signature of what's in the environment, positively or negatively.

Insight: Sammie, what does a refined soul matrix have to do with energetic sensitivity?

"From the perspective of soul, the human body is a vehicle to experience. The sensory system is the means to process energetic information, to inform the body what the human experience is. The number of 'spaces' available through the soul matrix enables a person to process more refined energy. I use the Spiritual Breath to process energetic information. It's also the means to communicate with Source what the soul expression, and the physical vehicle, experiences."

Autists & their Sensitive Sensory System

The sensory system receives energetic information from the environment. The human neurological system processes the information to make sense of this reality. Humanity co-creates reality as a collective based on what it's able to perceive. Consider that perceptually humanity perceives only three dimensions. Until the present day, humanity raised children based on the same 3D perceptions of reality. In this process, neuropathways were reinforced or numbed to function in 3D. This system of reality shaping (or programming) ensured that humanity remained cycling through a rigid 3D paradigm.

Those who could perceive beyond three dimensions often faced ridicule or worse, since they challenged accepted views of reality. Autists perceive way beyond what the 'normal human' perceives. 3D conformity programming narrows the bandwidth of energetic information and grossly misses the mark of the Autist's innate multidimensional awareness.

Mainstream education and therapies recognize that individuals with autism operate on a different sensory system. The treatments, however, focus on adapting their sensory systems to tolerate and adapt to function like the 3D human. Sammie received intensive early intervention and therapies since after medical diagnosis of autism. She would make short-term gains with heavy prompting and continuous external stimuli to refocus her. She would occasionally speak, but we'd never hear her say the uttered words again. Some days, she would unexpectedly explode and bang her head on the floor for unexplained reasons (inexplicable for us, anyway). This went on for years and she grew further away from the developmental 'norm.' Regardless of treatment and therapies, the imprint of the Spiritual Breath on Sammie's soul, was indelible. She's not here to be a 3D human.

Sammie senses energy at multidimensional levels, which include the 3D realm. To her, however, the outer 3D realm is but a snippet of reality. We view autists as dysfunctional compared to the 3D humans we know. From Sammie's perspective, the 3D human operates desensitized and in perpetual forgetfulness. She uses her sensory system to commune with God Source about her experiences. Like untainted eyes, Sammie and the Autists interface with Source to make energetic adjustments here on Earth to keep us on track for the Ascension.

"I process information using my omnipresence to align totally to Source." Spelled out by Sammie via letter board.

The Sensitivities of Autists as a Human Evolutionary Leap

Sammie, and the Autists, act as a prototype for the multidimensional and multi-sensory awake human. The Breath of Spirit imprinted this intention into her soul matrix. Attempts to re-program her via 3D education could not change this very fact.

The Autists, as a collective consciousness, function in the 7-12th dimensions. As individuals, their consciousness most coherently operates in the 7, 8, or 9th dimension. Sammie's consciousness operates coherently in the 8th dimension. The original angelic human blueprint or Avatar Human is 12 dimensional. Telepathic and energetic intelligence is part of humanity's divine blueprint. Sammie believes that the design of the human sensory system is to understand the diverse languages of God. For various reasons, humanity lost these abilities to communicate telepathically, energetically, and to understand the full 12 languages of Source. Collectively, the Autists act as a bridge to bring those higher dimensional blueprint layers back to humanity. This will exponentially advance, not just the human consciousness but the entire physical human.

In the past, ascended masters incarnated to assist humanity evolve. Unfortunately, while the human form and structure operated on dense 3D constructs, the spiritual teachings of ascension appeared outside of the physical reality humanity knew. Humans stuck in a 3D ego consciousness, distorted these advanced teachings.

The ascension mission cannot happen by just bringing through high vibrational concepts and spiritual ideas. The form and structure of the physical vessel also requires changes and adjustments to experience physically higher vibrational consciousness. Hence, the evolutionary aspect happens through the activations and corrections of the full DNA template that makes up the 12 dimensional Avatar Human.

Sammie and the Autists look dysfunctional from a 3D human perspective. In order for them to incarnate here, they connected to a very dense human form. It's like squeezing vastness into a container that is too small. As Autists, like Sammie, merge their collective consciousness with the 3D human they contribute to humanity's evolution. The Indigos, Starseeds, and New Children stabilize a 1 to 7 dimensional consciousness on the planet that merges with the 7 to 12 dimensional Autist consciousness. This accelerates the evolutionary leap of humanity. The union with the vast consciousness state of the Autists will eventually birth a different physical human than we know now.

Imagine a human race that consciously feels and senses the energy all around us. Lying, cheating, and hidden agendas could not exist because all would be aware of such nefarious acts. The New Earth will be based on authenticity and the power of the Oneness. The human will embody their God Self and be telepathic, clairsentient and eventually, omniscient.

The Ascension and evolution of humanity will span hundreds of years. This decade of 2020 is pivotal. At the time of this writing, humanity is witnessing the breakdown of 3D. Those who have held power and control over the planet are exerting great fear with the Corona virus. The Controllers fear the breakdown of their 3D reality, but they didn't count on these Autists interfering with their agenda. Or many awakening in the human collective.

Sammie and the Autist Collective work at multidimensional levels to keep this ascension mission on track. Unknown creation technologies in the form of energy symbols and activations stream through to help us adjust to the planetary and cosmic changes occurring. Sammie and I collaborate to bring through these creation technologies. This actualizes Sammie's soul work.

Each of us can make a difference.

Here are a few tips to connect with and support Autists:

- Presume competence. Respect who they are. Speak to them directly and know that they do understand what you're saying. Many considered nonverbal are writing books using new paradigm communication methods such as the Rapid Prompting Method (RPM, using letter boards) and Facilitated Communication (FC). Note that some "experts" and Wikipedia have very negative things to say about these modalities. Decide for yourselves after considering different success stories. Check out the numerous books written by Autists on Amazon.

- Practice deep breathing. In moments when an Autist becomes very anxious, loud and agitated, breathe deeply and bring yourself into a calm state. Center yourself in love and compassion. Teachers, aides, and therapists can help a whole classroom feel calmer this way.

- Invite them into your Meditation. To open to deeper communication with someone like Sammie, meditate holding his or her clothes or their blanket if you're a parent or caregiver. Sammie took me on many adventures this way. People have also told me she's shown up in their dreams. Other Autists have presented themselves to me spiritually.

- Be open to new perspectives. Notice your thoughts, visions, and feelings for a few hours or days. The Autists you know may have energetically spoken to you with new insights and ideas.

- Remove or decrease toxins in your home environment and in your food as much as possible. Essential oils in a diffuser is one simple method, and switching to natural cleaning products, and organic foods are a few options.

- Parents, be forgiving and compassionate to yourself. We did the best we could with what we knew. It's impossible to do everything regarding treatments, supplements, diets… Maintain balance with your finances and with the energy reserves you have. A stressful home environment also affects Autists.

Sammie and the Autists facilitate the ascension and evolution of Humanity

Sammie, and the Autists, incarnated for a very specific God-inspired purpose. Their sensory systems as awakened soul beings enable them to experience a deeper energetic communion with God. Society characterizes their sensory processing as 'dysfunctional.' Society's norms, systems, and paradigm platforms shaped by the limited 3D perceptions keep humanity looping in forgetfulness. Societal programming filters humanity's conscious and sensory experiences of God. Attempts to reprogram Sammie (and Autists) is impossible. They are physically incapable of "resonating" within being at an energetic level of consciousness that is not in total alignment with God Source. Autism, when viewed from an aspiring societal level, is not a dysfunction but a stimulating force designed to dismantle misaligned systems and beliefs that are not authentically soul-based. As humanity awakens to Soul embodiment, the outer systems and paradigms will change to reflect and mirror the inner divine authenticity, innate to the true Avatar Human. This is a multidimensional, revolutionary evolution. Sammie and others like her are here to serve humanity in ways unimaginable. They represent God Source's love for One Humanity.

Yemaya Renuka Duby

Yemaya Renuka Duby devoted the past 30 years to understand and contribute to the healing of people who suffered from childhood adversity and trauma. That journey which stemmed from her own need for empowerment and recovery took her across the planet, from Europe to the Americas, and around the Pacific ocean. She shared her heart offerings in many intentional communities, created 2 small healing centers and committed to build her wisdom through in-depth studies of the traditions of Somatic Therapy, Zen Buddhism, Yoga, Ayurveda and the Vedas, 5Rhytmns Dance, plant medicines, non-violent communication, Hula, Huna and more.

With her unique mixture of depth and lightness her current focus is to help women and men transform their relationships to grief and loss into a formidable initiation to reach their power, purpose and passion. This commitment is her contribution to bringing back the balance of the Feminine and Masculine energies on the planet and evolve our human

How to find out more about Yemaya:

Her website is: www.theembrace.life
https://www.instagram.com/theembrace.life
https://www.facebook.com/yemayarenuka

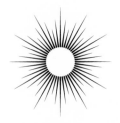

From Grief to Love:
Healing The Heart of Belonging

BY YEMAYA RENUKA DUBY

When I was a little girl, my mother disappeared suddenly, and I was left with my working father. At age 5, I learned to be alone, as alone as one can be. My father got me dogs. They became my brothers, my solace.

I learned to "be with what is" at such a young age. That opened the door to my ability to dive into pain instead of fleeing from it. Giving myself the permission to feel was the gift that transformed my life. It guided my path, as an evolutionary midwife of transformation, to those ready to liberate themselves from the shackles of emotional pain.

April 2020. We are in forced isolation

After two weeks working, studying and surfing online, I dive deeper into my internal being. I disconnect from WIFI and shut my cell phone off. I write. I write to you about grief. Grief does not scare me anymore. But I know it scares many. Most humans have a misconceived aversion to loss and it twists our relationship to grief.

For over 25 years I witnessed and facilitated ⨍
ers in my practice. I've seen it hiding under al͟
frozen by fear, guarded by anger, and distractᴇ
have to move grief and its many faces through ͟
we are ready to be free, whole, empowered and alig͟
unique purpose.

From Grief to Love: Tending to our Heart Garden

The heart is like a garden. It can grow weeds so thick, with thorns so protective, that parts of our inner landscape become accessible only to the worms and the bees, hopefully turning our past mistakes and suffering into honey, as author Paulo Coelho poetically suggests.

The heart is also like a castle with many chambers. Some chambers can be unknown to even the Queen or King of the castle. Locked shut, the doors to these chambers bar our entrance, the keys thrown God knows where.

When a visitor ventures down the labyrinth of our emotional intimacy, chasing after our inner child, glimpses of a path appear. But instead of having our longing to be at one with and loved by another deeply satisfied, we run away, lose our self and hide. We continue yearning for the day someone will reach the center of our castle, touch the heart of our longing, and transform it into Belonging.

This moment of shared glory rewards only those committed to the vulnerability of true intimacy. The muscles around most hearts have hardened. Covered with weeds and thorns, dark tapestries hide away the doors and the crevices the keys have fallen into.

We have to go through the body, to heal the heart and release unprocessed grief that lies behind our hidden doors. Only then can we experience true freedom, empowered choice and real intimacy. The muscles and fascia were the contractions and adhesions of trauma hide open under three actions:

ement, Vibration, Touch.

ovement: Dance, Yoga, Qi Gong, Running, Hiking...

Vibration: Sound, Breath, Frequencies...

Touch: Conscious bodywork, Massage, Energy work, Rosen Method, Trager, Tantra...

Choosing to shift the energy of held grief through movement, touch and vibrational therapy catalyzes our healing journey.

We have developed capacities to help us survive our traumatic experiences. Aside from flight, flight or freeze, we've also learned to numb ourselves. We numb with alcohol, tobacco, marijuana, food, sex, entertainment, shopping, over working or abusive relationships. This reinforces what we are numbing against.

We numb with muscle contractions that become "positionings". These kill our aliveness and vulnerability so that we can continue to function in a patriarchal world that does not have time or does not give a damn for our soul's expression. Shoulders come up and over to protect a broken heart, chests cave in to keep us from antagonizing a violent surrounding, hips turn in as an attempt to guard a sexual center under attack, pelvises stick up and back ready to put up a good fight. There are as many "positionings" as there are stories of pain and our diverse responses to the pain.

If you are an Empath, you have a harder time numbing. It's like you did not get the memo on self soothing. You have to buy stronger drugs or agree to become a "transitional character" -- the one who stops the family cycles of abuse and bravely heals. For most Empaths, it's not even a choice. It's: "transform that poison or die". "Become the Alchemist you were born to be or get locked up in a mental health facility!"

Healing trauma and grief is not a path for the faint of heart. You will need teachers, healers, mentors and angels. They will appear.

You will touch rage and sometimes a despair so deep that you might feel that you are walking close to madness. That will change.

You will discover a pulse of aliveness that will guide you and reveal the path deep through the bushes and thorns beyond the dark corner of your garden. Your awakened spirit will guide you through those castle corridors and take you to a chamber of your heart that, once open, will blast a light so bright you discover your pure essence underneath all the baggage you carried for years. Your essence is peace. Your essence is love. It is the place you will always return to. When you meditate. When you commune with Gaia.

This becomes your way of being. It becomes who you are.

Unwinding the Core

1991. I'm a 25-year-old living in a monastery. I'm hungry for peace and self-knowledge, and I want to deal with the anger that surfaces in my intimate relationships with men. I am a survivor of physical and emotional violence on one hand, and early childhood abandonment on the other. Both of my parents did their very best with what they had. Both are now beloved and forgiven. They gifted me with the entry to my life's work. Regardless of what occurred in my childhood, I committed to attain my full potential and to follow Life's invitation.

The relationship that came for me in the quietness of living in deep meditation had the power to surface my deepest wounds. One morning, I walked into the dining room, bent in two, walking like an arthritic 90-year-old woman. The tightness around my heart, so intense, that it was impossible for me to stand erect. Pain contorted my body, almost crippling me. I discovered a pamphlet about the Rosen Method of Somatic Therapy and Bodywork on the table where I sat. The rest is herstory.

My somatic therapy teacher, Marion Rosen declared: "Relaxation is the gateway to awareness." The methodology I learned under her care was like horse whispering for humans. I became a

25

muscle whisperer. I could gain any body's trust with the presence of my touch. Marion's method uses touch with hands that listen instead of manipulate. Once the connection of trust occurs, the hands soothe, invite, question, offer new choices and fully meet the body. And through the body, the heart and soul.

Imagine a frightened bird or a wild horse. The only instance when you will feel their body relax in your hand is when you are centered in a relaxed state of connection. Then you can reassure them energetically that you are not there to hurt them: you are respecting who they are, intrinsically. No matter how wild or how hurt they are, you are not there to change them. It's from that place of relaxed, connected, benevolent respect that magic can happen. The unwinding of the core gifts us with healing.

After three decades of deep diving into the mechanisms of Somatic Healing, deeply influenced by the Rosen Method, my clients evolution and my own healing journey to wholeness, I applied myself to translate and systemize the work beyond the need for physical touch. Out of this commitment surfaced my unique and current practice.

The Heart of Belonging

At the root of all feelings of pain and separation, failure and self-loathing, shame and fear and those of success and grace, pride and self-love, acceptance and connection is what I call the Heart of Belonging. When the Heart of Belonging has been damaged, smashed from violence and abuse, or hairline-fractured by contempt the Mind Body reorganizes itself around the wound, for efficiency and survival. In most cases of mended injuries, when the wound is not cleaned properly, it can fester. If the bones mis-align and the muscles are not reeducated with physical therapy, one loses range of motion.

Emotional injuries work the same way. We see brilliant, hard-working humans, not able to attain their financial goals, because at the core of their Heart of Belonging, there is unprocessed pain.

We see fabulous, gorgeous, loving beings not able to land the intimate relationship they long for because at the center of their Heart of Belonging, the mind and body hold old beliefs. These lodge so deeply, with teeth and claws so sharp that only a deeply committed team, consisting of the mentor and the mentee—sometimes one and the same—can find the entrance and key that will unravel the knot to freedom.

Individuals often forget important elements essential to the success of our healing journey. As a practitioner and as a survivor, I can not imagine recovery without the solidity of sacred space and the importance of integration. Omitting these raises alarming suspicion that the formula used is faulty or that the progress initiated could backlash into a new traumatic experience.

When we learn the art of bending or transforming reality, known as Magic, we must create "sacred space". A strong container of sacred space can hold potent magic. A flimsy one can invite trouble. As a healer you need to know how to create a strong container. For your one-on-one sessions or for your hundred people live rituals, the energetic space must be in place to provide potency, clarity, energetic cleanliness and safety. These are important for your healing mission, for your participants, for yourself and for the location you are using. If you are a new practitioner, I deeply recommend that you look for help and learn how to create a strong container for your work. And if you are experienced, I recommend you stay aware. It's not a good idea to get sloppy with the Sacred. It can cause more pain than good and come back to bite you when you least expect it.

Integration with Gaia, The Earth

Hiking is great medicine. It offers two of the fundamental components of healing: breath and movement. It clears the head and fosters integration of our daily organic contractions and expansions. We tune in to the gifts of Gaia, our Mother, our Shelter, and Queen. When we can be fully present with Her bounty, we achieve

Oneness with everything… And Her winds reminds you that you are limitless.

When we open our heart to healing, through therapeutic inner work or conscious intimate relationships, we often fear tapping into the pain that lives in our deeper chambers. The more light shines in, the less space is available for our hidden trauma experiences. If we trust the process and ride our **Oceanic Inner Feeling Wave**—a built-in organic physiological mechanism—we can be present with the deepest, most excruciating pain and get back to a "safe-shore" in a matter of a few minutes.

Our resistance to re-experiencing the pain of the past is where we get caught. That Fear Zone is where we get into serious trouble. It can be like a typhoon that never spits us out. Neither in nor out. Such endless spinning can seriously damage our nervous, endocrine and adrenal systems. It can create severe depression and keep us from expressing rage in a healthy way. However, if we surrender completely, we can move through to the other side of the pain, into peace and integration.

Riding the **Oceanic Inner Feeling Wave** allows transformation of held emotion into grace. Once the body of a wild horse, scared bird or skittish dog reaches a point of trust that allows the release of past trauma, the body shakes, cries or trembles. Then it breathes. It breathes deep. The open space inside a full breathing body is where gentle transformation of our relationship to loss, death and separation happens. Like a snake shedding its skin, we need to trust into the release of what we know, embracing the unknown and invisible, before we truly emerge anew.

Regulating our dives within and implementing integration are essential steps in our healing journey to wholeness and freedom. Since the heart is a muscle, its inherent movement is to open and contract continuously. Some of us, spiritual people and young hippies wishfully think to keep their hearts open at all times. Highly evolved beings can stay at peace amid pain or deep triggers. I, myself, aspire to open with the entirety of my being—to both pain and love. To one living this Earth journey to embrace the unbear-able lightness of being the fullest of her experience, musters in genuine surrender. This is the next level of commitment I invite our culture to.

Let's release our fear of death and stop trying to control our life and the pain that is an inherent part of our human journey. Let's bravely experience grief, loss, and any other uncomfortable feel-ing. Not in acceptance or permissiveness of senseless acts of vio-lence, but on the contrary, in the daring welcoming of unrewarded acts of beauty. For us to come to these places we need to befriend our **Oceanic Inner Feeling Wave** and give ourselves and each other the permission to feel. Once we trust the ebb and flow within our feeling body, we become adept emotional surfers; we stand fully in the heart's power and work in harmony with the living planet which is patiently hosting us.

Dr. Karen kan

Dr. Karen Kan is a medical doctor and Doctor of Light Medicine. As the founder of the TOLPAKAN™ Healing Method, "Dr. Karen" has discovered through her own journey of recovering from fibromyalgia, chronic fatigue syndrome, autoimmune disease and depression, that these issues are more common and more difficult to treat in highly sensitive people. Given that approximately 20% of people are highly sensitive according to research, Dr. Karen's mission is to help sensitive souls harness their sensitivity as a Superpower, fulfill their purpose, and create a life of joy. In her live events and online programs, Dr. Karen trains highly sensitive people how to tap into their intuitive abilities, healing abilities and manifesting abilities.

Dr. Karen works with sensitive souls such as indigos, earth angels, starseeds, empaths, walk-ins and ET-human hybrids, helping them understand who they are, why they are here and how they chose to experience this incarnated lifetime. In her TOLPAKAN™ Healing Method Level 1 Training Program, she empowers people to ALIGN with the Divine, ASK quality questions, and ACTIVATE high vibrational healing energies.

You can find out more about Dr. Karen Kan here:

Her website is https://www.karenkan.com/
https://www.facebook.com/groups/lightwarriornetwork
https://www.youtube.com/user/karenkanmd

ALTERNATE-SELF SYNDROME:
HOW HIGHLY SENSITIVE PEOPLE CAN HEAL MULTIPLE TIMELINES TO CREATE GREATER HEALTH AND WELLNESS

BY DR. KAREN KAN

"GERTRUDE" WAS AN ELDERLY family member of one of my patients. She kept telling her family that she was seeing multiple versions of her husband. She also saw people in all manner of clothing traipsing through her home and property. Some looked as if they came from the television show, The Little House on the Prairie, and some looked like they were alien humanoids dressed like the people from the movie, The Hunger Games. These people kept showing up out of nowhere and she kept yelling at them to get off her property. Her doctors diagnosed her with dementia and put her on medications. They didn't help much.

My patient asked me to do an intuitive reading on Gertrude. To my surprise, I discovered that what Gertrude was seeing was real. Her geographical location housed certain unusual characteristics. Multiple timelines and dimensions were easily accessible, and

Gertrude was experiencing a profound opening of her clairvoyant gifts. She was highly sensitive. Unfortunately, I didn't work with her directly to recalibrate her gifts so she wouldn't have to suffer anxiety from seeing multiple realities simultaneously.

In this chapter, I share with you a phenomenon, not unlike what Gertrude was experiencing, that occurs with many people worldwide without them knowing it. I call it the *Alternate-Self Syndrome*.

Highly sensitive people often suffer from unusual or challenging symptoms, some relating to issues arising from their alternate lives. The great news is that Light Medicine can rectify these symptoms easily.

If you are highly sensitive, you might notice that:

You feel terrible around negative people

Noise, bright lights, and crowds bother you

You are highly intuitive and creative

Traditional medications don't work well

You have environmental allergies and intolerances

Have you been criticized, ostracized, or medicalized for your sensitivity? If you have, it's common and you are not alone.

What if sensitivity is a Superpower?

Being highly sensitive may seem like a burden because you can't act like a normal person. What is okay and tolerable for a regular person to experience is often stressful to you if you are highly sensitive. Maybe you were told by well-meaning family and friends to "toughen-up", "grow thicker skin", or "just stop being so sensitive!" Maybe you felt like you needed fixing.

But I'm here to tell you that there is nothing wrong with you. Just because you react violently to pesticides, food colorings, chemicals, cell phones, Wi-Fi and other man-made inventions, does not make you abnormal. It makes you gifted.

You are not the problem. You are the solution.

Wha????

Okay, let me back up a bit here. Every single highly sensitive person who I've worked with is a special soul who consciously incarnated in a human body for the purpose of elevating the love, light and consciousness of this planet as a volunteer. If you are reading this book, then you are one of them.

Does that make you more gifted than the average person? Yes, in some respects it does, but it is more accurate to say that you've already activated your gifts and are evolving faster than non-sensitives.

The actual problem you've had is not understanding who you truly are and not knowing how to hone your gifts so you can enjoy them. You've been suffering because no one trained you on what to do when you *feel too much*. Your ability to feel is your intuition.

Your tendency to feel too much is your intuition on overload. It's like possessing the most sophisticated radar on the planet that can pick up energies from the very minute, quantum level to the very ginormous, cosmic level, but no instruction manual to show you how to scan only for the information you want, rather than everything. Just imagine how much energetic data you're picking up every day with no way of organizing it or making sense of it.

What does this have to do with your alternate lives?

Plenty. Let me explain more.

Over the last several years, our Universe has been going through a rapid expansion process many people call The Ascension. When I talk about ascension, I'm not talking about traditional religions. It's an evolutionary process. Because I am a Sensitive; I have experienced recurring jumps in energy I've nicknamed Ascension Upgrades. These jumps can happen a few times a week or several times a day. Over the last few years, these upgrades have been intense and everyone has felt major shifts in their lives.

Sudden deaths, marriage break-ups, change in careers, or change in locales are often also the result of the ascension process.

Ascension upgrades can be very intense and if a person hasn't cleared old low-vibrational baggage, whether that be their own or ancestral, the healing detoxification effects can make someone sick. Some people even die.

Sensitive souls committed to their spiritual evolution often go through a unique discomfort. Although they also detoxify on all levels, the largest discomfort caused by the Ascension Process is the expansion of their spiritual gifts.

With the expansion of spiritual gifts, highly sensitive people are more aware of other timelines and dimensions. They expand beyond their five senses. Their sensitivity radar increases. Their abilities to heal and manifest increase. Some people call it a Spiritual Awakening. Other people call it a nightmare because suddenly they see, hear, or feel things foreign to them, such as ghosts, demons, angels, and extraterrestrials.

Other phenomena occur with Ascension. One is that our timelines have *converged*. What it means for you is that the boundaries between past, present, future, parallel and non-parallel lives have become thin. It's like everything is collapsing into the NOW. On the one hand, it means that we can heal all of our lives simultaneously! On the other, symptoms from our other timelines can leak or bleed into this one. When it happens, it can make us feel a little crazy or sometimes sick.

Francine, a long-time client of mine, came into the office one day with shocking news. Hospitalized her for a mild heart attack, she had few risk factors for heart disease other than being overweight. She had absolutely no signs or symptoms prior to this attack. When her doctor checked her coronary arteries, the blood vessels feeding blood to the heart, none of them were seriously clogged.

Her doctors were scratching their heads about why she ended up with a heart attack.

Using Divine Muscle Testing™ we determined the foundational reason for her condition. Francine experienced a heart attack in another timeline. Because her timelines converged physically, not dimensionally, the way it should, she experienced symptoms *leaking* into this reality. Understanding this was a case of Alternate-Self Syndrome, we recalibrated the timeline convergence and minimized the negative effects to her physical body.

Francine healed rapidly, and a few weeks later her doctors confirmed that there was no trace of damage to her heart. It was as if she had never suffered a heart attack. She discontinued all of her medications and returned to being active and productive.

What if your unexplained symptoms of pain, allergies, or autoimmunity are because of Alternate-Self Syndrome?

The Alternate-Self Support Protocol can help you deal with Alternate-Self Syndrome. It uses TOLPAKAN™ Healing (TKH) Method Directives, an intention-focused technique to direct specific healing frequencies. Most people are attuned to these frequencies. For you to use them effectively, it's just a matter of focused attention and practice.

Alternate-Self Support Protocol

The first directive recalibrates timeline convergence to minimize symptoms leaking or bleeding into this timeline. The second directive restores sovereignty to your boundaries. The third directive rebalances your spiritual gifts, which include your expanded abilities to see (clairvoyance), hear (clairaudience), feel (clairsentience), smell (clairessence), taste (clairgustience), and know (claircognisance).

Before you say these TKH Directives, find a quiet place where you can be alone and undisturbed so you can experience these with your undivided attention. I recommend my STOIM™ technique (*stillness through observing internal movement*) to bring all your energy into the present moment.

Rub your hands together vigorously for several seconds. Then stop, close your eyes, and focus on the vibration and energy inside your body.Feel the flow of energy and follow what happens inside, without judgement or expectation. Congratulations! You've just done STOIM.

Once you've spent upwards of a minute in this space, open your eyes gently, and say each of these directives out loud while noticing what happens to the flow of energy within.

TKH Directive #1: Recalibrate Convergence

"I now command that all my timelines converge in the optimal way and remove, dissolve and uncreate any discomfort or symptoms leaking or bleeding into this timeline in the highest and best way, all directions in time, with ease, speed and grace. Thank you."

TKH Directive #2: Restore Boundaries

"I now command that all my boundaries; physical, mental, emotional, energetic, spiritual, dimensional and relational, restore to 100% sovereign, in the highest and best way, all directions in time, in all timelines where I exist, with ease, speed and grace. Thank you."

TKH Directive #3: Rebalance Gifts

"I now command that all my sensitivity gifts balance to 100% in all directions of time, in all timelines where I exist, in the highest and best way, with ease, speed and grace. Thank you."

In my experience, these TKH Directives work very well in about 85% of people suffering from Alternate-Self Syndrome. You only need to do the Recalibrate Convergence Directive once. Because of ascension upgrades, I recommend doing the Restore and Rebalance Directives daily to keep sensitivity symptoms controlled.

Please note that it is common to feel relaxed or sleepy the first time you do these directives. Many people feel calmer and lighter.

If these directives don't seem to work for you, you might not be experiencing Alternate-Self Syndrome or you might need to understand what the causes are before symptoms can resolve. Sometimes, getting expert help in investigating the foundational causes of your symptoms is the quickest way to resolving the issues.

As a sensitive soul, you are spiritually gifted! Because of the naturally occurring Ascension process, your gifts expand. Without awareness of these phenomena or training to help you manage these gifts, you might experience uncomfortable symptoms. You may experience Alternate-Self Syndrome where symptoms leak from one timeline into another. The Alternate-Self Support Protocol is a TOLPAKAN™ Healing Method to help you reduce symptoms and restore balance. By doing the Restore and Rebalance Directives daily, you'll experience greater ease and comfort.

GWEN LEPARD

GWEN LEPARD IS A Radiant Relationship Luminary who lights the way to self-love, joy and worthiness. As a Baggage Begone™ Mentor, and Speaker, she helps Empaths who've experienced narcissistic abuse overcome their relationship baggage, optimize self-love and own their personal power so that they can have the love, peace and freedom they desire. What she's really passionate about is creating Radiant Relationships that stand the test of time.

She has a presence that inspires others to live a more open, genuine life with gratitude, self-love, and compassion.

Among her modalities are Energy Medicine Practitioner, Success Strategist, Master Hypnotherapist, NLP Master Practitioner, and Quantum Jumping. She's an International Speaker, Award Winning Broadcaster and Co-Author of the books, *The Gratitude Book Project* and *Pure Genius*. She has appeared on the Life Transformation Summit, From Heartache to Joy, You Wealth Revolution, and Light Warrior Radio Show.

"We carry residue from relationships that block wellness, wealth, love, and our success. As a guide-by-the-side it's a joy to help Empaths remove that residue."

How to find out more about Gwen Lepard:

Her website is www.gwenlepard.com
facebook.com/groups/BaggageBegone
Her email address is: support@gwenlepard.com

COURAGEOUS COMPASSION:
HOW EMPATHS EVOLVE OUT OF NARCISSISSTIC ABUSE

BY GWEN LEPARD

"THE TRANSFORMATION JOURNEY IS not for the faint of heart. It is for those courageous souls willing to look within. This journey requires compassion to soothe the inner voices. It requires Courageous Compassion!"

This evolution begins with a willingness to choose the path less travelled, no matter what the consequences, and to do so with awareness, kindness, and the understanding that you've made a conscious choice.

In this chapter, you'll find characteristics of Narcissists and Empaths, three tactics that narcissists use to enslave Empaths, and three steps to becoming an Empowered Empath. These practices shifted me out of a pattern that attracted an abusive narcissistic husband, a business partner with similar traits, and a covert narcissist that finally shook me out of my self-protective walls and pushed me into my full-blown empathic gifts.

My former husband displayed the characteristics of narcissism. He hid his deep sense of insecurity under a facade of bravado, charm, and egotism. Narcissism is a mental health issue that drives those that suffer from it to demoralize and tear down others. Studies show the reason that narcissists are devoid of compassion is that their brains are malformed in the area that creates empathy. There is no remedy for this deformity.

It's easy for a narcissist to entice an Empath. As an Empath, you want to heal their emotional pain because you feel it. If you're an unaware Empath, you're a people pleaser to your own detriment. A narcissist uses your need for validation as a tool to control you. He or she will say the things you want to hear to keep you under their spell. They do everything they can to continue feeding off your life force. You believe that you're the one that can heal the narcissist. What happens instead, is that you engage in a victim/victimizer dance.

As an Empath that hasn't yet owned your power, you present a smorgasbord for hungry narcissists. Having your very being distorted, demeaned, and drained is only an infinitesimal fraction of what it's like to experience narcissistic abuse. This form of abuse is a spiritual injury. What is fascinating is that underlying that injury is the little-known role of the narcissist. Want to know this truth? Okay then… It is to push the Empath into the awakening of their gifts.

Disempowered To Empowered

I see a lot of anger in people that have experienced narcissistic abuse. While it's entirely understandable, this anger is another form of disempowerment. Studies show long-held anger can be detrimental to your overall well-being. There are those who want to hang onto victimhood. They will scream, "victim-blaming" and cling to the pain as it validates their current experience.

It's true. Think about it. A victim is the virtuous one, holding no responsibility, and receiving sympathy. If you define yourself by the victimization of experience, remember disempowered Empaths feed narcissists. If you're ready to leave victimhood behind and step into your true power and gifts, then read on...

You can go from a disempowered Empath to an empowered Empath. Use the three steps in this chapter to evolve out of the state that turns you into a narcissist's dinner, and you can welcome the gifts that are yours to command. As you awaken, your natural ability to heal becomes stronger. Your manifestation powers increase exponentially. You develop the capacity to set clear and healthy boundaries. Opportunities for you to create income doing what you love show up out of the blue. Your physical energy increases and you have more zest for life!

We're all energy balls bumping around and overlapping into each other's energy fields. When a narcissist finds an Empath that is wide open and giving from their enormous heart, they'll plug into that field and start draining the Empath energetically. This draining can cause brain fog, confusion, and deep, unexplained exhaustion.

The Three Tactics That Narcissists Use To Enslave Empaths

These tactics are attachments, addiction, and approval.

Attachments are energetic control tools placed in your energy field, and they show up in many forms. You may have heard of cords and cord-cutting. I see them as shackles. They show up in various forms of restraining devices I help clients remove. Collars, corsets, cages, and chastity belts are a few of the energetic attachments that bind you to someone parasitic like an energy vampire or a narcissist.

Addiction can show up as trauma bonds, dependence, and codependency. Often there is the satisfaction of the "need to be needed." This is a big component found in the Empath/Narcissist dance. As a disempowered Empath, you'll put up with abuse, insults, humiliation, and more to feel needed. A narcissist will happily let you feel needed while taking your very life essence and vitality.

Often there is a physical component of addiction. I was in a relationship with a covert narcissist and didn't even know it. His ability to use self-serving empathy worked well as a cover. It wasn't until he sent me a "love-bomb" email, using "love" to change what I felt about a betrayal, that I realized that I had missed all the signs of narcissism in him.

There were strong physical and emotional addictions in that relationship. I mentioned "self-serving empathy." He used it to create a feedback loop of "feeling me, feeling him, feeling me!" It was an intoxicating experience, and I accepted things that were completely outside of my core values to have that feedback loop in my life. It took an extreme betrayal to break the ties that had me repeatedly going back to him.

Approval and your need for it, in this Narcissist/Empath dance, becomes a means to control you. When you seek validation, are stuck in victim mentality, or are unaware of your value, it's easy for a narcissist to manipulate you for their "feeding" needs. They use this desire for acceptance and twist it, using Gaslighting to further enslave you.

Gaslighting is an insidious form of abuse as it invalidates all your senses so you no longer trust yourself. It is one of the favorite tools of narcissists. They sow doubt by telling you one thing and then denying it. Narcissists use Gaslighting to weaken and manipulate you, by denying your truths, facts, and even your environment. Eventually, they will have you questioning everything in your reality. When looking to a narcissist for approval, you get the opposite: low self-esteem, anxiety, and the feeling that everything you do is wrong.

How Do You Evolve Out Of Abuse That Can Have You Question Your Very Existence?

If you need to know why something happened to you, why someone did what they did. Why, why, why??... I have an answer for you that may shift you out of victim programming.

Somewhere, some part of your Soul said, "Yes," to what you experienced. Ultimately, that experience was for your highest good, even if it didn't seem like it at that moment. Gaining awareness of the permission your soul granted to experience brutal abuse is key to evolving out of victimhood.

During this journey out of narcissistic abuse, there might be times when you feel that you're all alone. I want you to know that you're never alone. There is support all around you including angels, ascended masters, and pure light beings. They need you to be courageous enough to ask for their help. If you feel that you've already done an enormous amount of work on your healing journey and you're not getting the results you want, there are three reasons. The first one is that the Divine has something better planned for you. The second reason is there is some benefit to you in the current situation, and the third is because it's not yet time for the results you desire to be manifested.

Please know that you're enough and have compassion for yourself as the beautiful child of the Universe you are. You're a miracle and all that has happened to you makes you even more of a miracle. Acceptance of the Yes and that "You Are Enough", with a willingness to be gentle with yourself, will move you into releasing resistance so you can receive the healing that you desire.

Three Steps To Becoming An Empowered Empath

How you evolve from the disempowered "dinner" of narcissists to owning your awakened gifts.

Step One: Remove The Shadow Cloak Of Responsibility

As an Empath, you feel responsible for healing others. This responsibility comes from feeling their pain. As a disempowered Empath, you attempt to heal everyone in your life. Typically, you take this on inappropriately. When you attempt to heal others without their permission, you not only take away the gifts and lessons from their journey, you take on their karma. Taking on another's karma shows up as a shadow cloak that is attached to your energy field. I call this form of attachment the Shadow Cloak of Responsibility.

You can remove this attachment and release the energy tying you to an abuser. The first step is awareness. There is an energetic shadow cloak attached to you from everyone that you have attempted healing. It's like it is sewn on to your energy field and it's draining you just by its existence.

Recognize that healing everyone, especially a narcissist, is NOT your responsibility. A wise quote says, "The only person you're responsible for is yourself. Everyone has their own journey to fulfill."

Move into acceptance that you've chosen the responsibility of healing another willingly and that you have the power to remove the resulting shadow cloak. Then you use energy medicine and visualization to disconnect and eliminate the attachment. This is a process that you can find in my *Empowered Empath Evolution* online course that results in you gaining your wings.

Step Two: Regain Rapport With Yourself

Rapport is a powerful tool that you use all the time to feel connected with others. However, as a disempowered empath it's entirely possible that you're disconnected from yourself. When you regain connection to yourself, you reveal your congruent inner power and can see your value.

In your unconscious, there are a vast number of parts that make up who you are as a personality. These parts have been created to protect you during significant experiences in your life. Some segments can conflict with others or be running incompatible programs that are now actually causing harm.

Integrating fragmented parts of the unconscious mind is an entire body of work. It's best done with someone that is skilled and trained in how to talk with these different fragments. It is one of the many modalities in my Lepard Method™ of working with clients.

Step Three: Reconnect To Your Radiance

You access your radiance through practicing self-love. Use the following three practices regularly to change your vibration. Your new frequency will make you immune to narcissists' enslavement tactics.

From Victim To Victorious - First Self Love Practice:

You can change your state using your body. I remember one of my trainers explaining this exercise. I'll walk you through it and you can follow along.

- Start crunching up your body.
- Roll your shoulders forward.
- Hunch your back.
- Tighten your abdominal muscles.
- Notice that you're barely breathing.
  Notice how you're feeling. pretty disempowered, right?
- Now...
- Sit up straight.
- Roll your shoulders back.
- Take a deep breath.
- Smile.

- Move your arms up into the "victory" V that you see many athletes do at the finish line.

- Notice how you feel now. Much more empowered, right!

This shift happened in a matter of seconds. You changed your state in seconds!

Eye Gazing - Second Self Love Practice:

I was first given this practice by a coach that challenged me to gaze into a mirror, look into my eyes, and say "I love you" or "I love me" for three minutes. It seemed like an eternity. I challenge you to just start and do it for however long you can. Doing this changed my life from insecure, desperate, and clingy, into strong, confident, and knowing of my worth. When I forget, I go back to the mirror exercise. Now you have this tool to use for your empowerment.

Self Holding - Third Self Love Practice:

This self-love practice of holding will give you oxytocin, the love hormone, that activates when you connect, hug, or cuddle with others. This is especially nice since, as Empaths, we need times of isolation for healing. Giving yourself oxytocin can help with that healing process.

Here is a simple presence and awareness practice. Put your hands on either side of your face. Cup your cheeks. Feel what it feels like to be present with yourself. Lean into one side and then the other. Hold your face like you would want a lover to hold it. Feel the temperature between your face and hands. Allow this to be a very loving touch. You can also wrap your arms around yourself. Place your hands on the opposite arms or shoulders and give yourself a squeeze.

Sometimes you just need to hold yourself and realize that you're the first healer and the one constant in your life. Yes, it's important to get support along the way and you're the ultimate authority on you! You can evolve out of narcissistic abuse, or any abuse. You are more powerful than you know. You now have some steps, tips, and tools to activate courageous compassion in your life.

Your gifts awaken for a purpose: to heal yourself. As you heal yourself, you heal others. You are courageous enough to have compassion for yourself, your journey, and those who have contributed to it along the way.

AADHYA DEVI

AADHYA DEVI IS AN emotional alchemist who has helped many women discover their inner truth, learn to heal their connection between their heart and their mind and unleash their feminine power by learning to self heal and live fully Unleashed, Untamed, and Unapologetic no matter their faith, creed, or culture.

The Inner Goddess Project was birthed from her personal experience of deep emotional pain and trauma which thrust her on her path towards personal healing, re-awakening the call to revive the suppression of the Goddess-Consciousness.

Charged with the task of re-awakening the deep feminine soul to humanity and earth, she uses her gifts as a seer and healer to help women activate their sacred intuitive-based codes within their personal grid, tear down the strongholds which steadfastly guard and block their heart, and activate the anesthetized kundalini life-giving force and sustaining power which has been suppressed for several millennia.

Aadhya not only helps her clients heal their deepest wounds, but she empowers them by teaching them how to connect directly to Source and to their Inner Being, freely accessing their holy template in moments of deep vulnerability and pain, centering them back to their heart. And like alchemy, her clients leave never the same.

How to find out more about Aadhya Devi:

Her website is: www.aadhyadevi.com
https://www.facebook.com/TheInnerGoddessProject
https://www.youtube.com/c/TheInnerGoddessProject
https://innergoddessproject.podbean.com/
https://www.instagram.com/theinnergoddessproject/

Becoming 5D:
The Human Journey of
Ascension and Rebirth

BY AADHYA DEVI

THERE IS A RHYTHM and flow to how creative energy moves. Its form is electric and magnetic. Its flow is wild and sensual. Its intention is to experience all realities for the purpose of expansion. And not long ago, in a moment of stillness and complete presence, this Creative Power (Source consciousness) thought how wonderful and expansive it would be to experience life in human form. And so, the human body was created. Source energy fashioned the human body to serve as a physical vessel for consciousness to interface with, in order to experience what it is like to create in a dense form.

Many of you reading this right now come from a diversity of culture, socioeconomic background, and faith which has directly influenced your perspective around life, purpose, and spirituality. But for a moment, could you consider setting aside your beliefs around faith and examine the possibility that perhaps we have missed something of greater importance? Something that has nothing to do with religion and has the power to bridge the gap between science and spirituality. Something that once learned will forever change your conscious experience on earth.

In this chapter, I will touch briefly on what your 4 bodies are, the structures and systems within your 4 bodies, what makes up your electromagnetic systems, how each one interfaces with one another, and why balance between all systems is so important. I am diving deeper into each of these systems in my book, however; I felt it was important to do my best to provide you with a brief overview on each one of these structures in this chapter as it is playing a major role in our ascension process. I will also touch on why trauma affects your spirit's ability to interface with the physical body, and how when you begin to heal your distortions and imbalances you begin to ascend and become 5D!

In this moment, our human form is upgrading to 5D. All structures and the way each structure interfaces with one another are drastically changing. If you are ready to take the leap into Becoming 5D and a conscious master creator, then it is important to understand how the spirit lives, functions, and thrives in the body. Your relationship between your body and spirit determines how well your spirit interfaces with the body. Your health and wellness of this connection affects what your spirit experiences and how it experiences reality in your matrix system. When your connection becomes corrupt, your body becomes imbalanced and will manifest disease, illness, and chaos. This imbalance directly affects your ability to create consciously, receive messages from higher guidance, and access Universal knowledge and tools. It robs you from integrating all systems to access 5D consciousness and beyond.

You were created with four bodies. These are your spiritual, mental, emotional, and physical body. The divine masculine governs your mental and physical body. The divine feminine governs your emotional and spiritual body. Each body has its own system and function, and when balanced can fully interface with the others. Your mental body governs and regulates your nervous system, biochemistry, and its construct is electric in nature. Your emotional body governs and regulates your meridians, chakras, biochemistry and is magnetic in nature. Think about it. The heart's magnetic field is the strongest rhythmic field that the body produces. There are other magnetic fields in the physical body that your body produces, and we will go into those shortly. But for now, know this. The heart's magnetic field is over 100 times greater in strength than the field generated by your brain and has been scientifically detected to project up to 3 feet away from the human body. The hearts magnetic field "envelopes" each cell in your body. That's pretty insane to think that each cell is bathed in its own magnetic field. And this magnetic field is connected to all circuitry in your biological system.

Your magnetic field contains coded information that travels through your nervous system. This electrical activity travels through your biological system and regulates your biochemistry. It will signal a response in your biochemistry and cause a hormonal and chemical reaction within your body. While your heart is releasing and pumping these hormones and chemicals into your body with each contraction, you trigger an emotional response. Your emotions release more chemicals and hormones. As all of this information is flooding the circuitry in your body, energy begins to flow through your meridians. The energy flowing through your meridians will begin to spin through your chakras in a spiral motion pulsating matching vibrational energy outward into your electromagnetic field. This electro-magnetic energy flows outward into the Universe and whichever force is an electromagnetic match to what you are emitting, through attraction, magnetizes its way towards you. That is the science and art of becoming 5D!

In a 5D experience, you are more connected to your inner being and can interface better with other's magnetic field. This advanced technology allows you to interface with another individual in a way that the connection and data you are receiving is clearer and more intimate. Your empathic abilities open and strengthen. When connected to the 5D matrix, you can connect your electromagnetic field with other species electromagnetic field such as dogs, cats, and wildlife. The more you become familiar with how your systems work together, you become better at interpreting the data you receive through your geometric grid system. Your geometric system and electromagnetic field operate as one. Your physical body tunes in with your environment and you can receive messages from Mother Gaia. You access the gifts you were born with, such as the ability to connect with those who have crossed over, the ability to see auras, past lives, or access the Akashic records. You begin to tap into multi-dimensional and Universal information, tools, and use these to retrieve data around possibilities for your future and what roadblocks may lie ahead. The electromagnetic field processes all of this data through it.

In all honesty, although as a species we have genetically evolved, we have yet to tap into the possibilities that await for us when we have fully accessed our personal grid. For thousands of years we have had the ability to connect to this technology and utilize these tools. However, over the last few thousand years, patriarchal, controlling forces severed our connection to this technology through suppressing the divine feminine. Through trauma, they extinguished our connection to this life force and corrupted our connection to our inner being. Until we learn to heal our core wounds and realign all our structures, we will continue to live out of balance.

When trauma occurs, it disturbs the electromagnetic communication between all systems. It creates physical density within the body. Density affects your ability to raise your vibration, which is necessary to activate your light body. Trauma creates stuck energy or blocks in your chakra system, which influences how well-balanced energy travels through your meridians. Your chakras and meridians are a function of your magnetic systems. Your meridians are pathways within your biology which are channels in which all energy in your body travels through. 80% of your energy is created through breath. It is through breath your electromagnetic grid is charged. Remember, there is scientifically measurable electricity in the air that you breathe.

Your chakras have many functions within its system. When I speak of the chakra systems, I am referring to how each individual chakra functions on its own. For example, each chakra can trigger a physical response such as a tight throat. This would indicate a person's throat chakra is blocked and that individual could have possibly experienced a loss of power to speak their truth. Chakras are a part of your bio-psychic energy system. They expose your emotional constitution, repressed feelings, and reveal the distortions you may have around past trauma and relationships. This energy system will inform you when you are in alignment or out of alignment. Chakras reveal your ability to create and love; and governs your access to divine guidance. Interpreting this data is important because it helps you determine how you are distributing energy within your field and how well balanced that distribution is.

Try to look beyond the religious perspective of chakras and look at them from a scientific viewpoint that perceives them as part of your biology; specifically, your magnetic structure. In science there are two types of currents. Direct current and alternating current. The human body's energy system is a direct current. Which means it flows in one direction. Now you know what your 4 bodies are, the structures and systems within your 4 bodies, what makes up your electromagnetic systems, how each one interfaces with one another, and why balance between all systems is so important. Let's discuss how trauma affects your spirit's ability to interface with the physical body. And how healing your distortions will bring balance between your systems and assist you in ascending to 5D!

Before we dive into how trauma affects your spirit's ability to interface with the physical body, I wanted to share a writing I wrote called "The Seed of Shame". This writing will provide deep insight to how we nurture distortions in our inner and outer world and how we suppress the Divine Feminine through trauma. I want to share this with you because I feel after you read it, you will better understand how healing the Divine Feminine is essential to ascension. And how when you heal the Divine Feminine, it will heal your electromagnetic field and all systems and functions within. When an individual is fully connected to their divine feminine, they stand authentically in their power. They can fully embody their inner being and freely express themselves in deep vulnerability. As you read this writing, know that I use the feminine pronouns to connect the reader's perspective with the intimate embodiment of the feminine energy that exists in all humans.

The Seed of Shame

"Shamed. Silenced. Oppressed. Anesthetized. The awakened feminine soul, life-giving force and sustaining power enslaved by the fear of man. She is forced into subservient humiliation when she dares to trustingly and freely expresses her vigor, radiance, and sensual passion confidently in moments of deep vulnerability. Then, the very subjugation of that victimization causes her to retreat inwardly. Layer by layer, building her walls up high. A mighty fortress, fortifying her safely within. Brick by brick, she stacks them high. Its fabric fashioned of judgement, criticism, and shame, ensuring the foundation to this impregnable fortress is reliable and predictable in perpetuity.

Destructively, she spreads the seeds of shame generously on her fertile soil. And once shame has rooted itself deeply and strongly into the core of her being, it yields fruit in abundance. And like all other fields of which are nurtured with care consistently and faithfully, its fruit becomes ripe for harvest. With great satisfaction, each laborer consumes the return of its harvest, giving life force and sustaining power in exchange for its next yield of production.

Reliable. Faithful. Acceptable. Dependable. Unquestionably, the individual will sever its connection to the Divine Feminine and will faithfully assimilate its will to suppress, condition, and extinguish its own light-force. That is the power, corruption, and promise of the Seed of Shame." - Aadhya Devi.

From the moment of birth, we are conditioned to nurture disconnection to our inner being. We are taught to doubt ourselves and mistrust our inner guidance system, which helps us to perceive how the outer world is influencing our inner world. This leads to imbalances in our energy field. In consequence we create distortions around who we think we are, what we think we deserve, and how we think we should be. Through these distortions, our connection between our heart and mind becomes corrupt. We navigate through life with an altered and skewed lens. Each trauma only adds to that distortion, creating a separation between our mind and heart. That is why you hear many healers speak of the importance of healing your past, reconnecting back to your inner being, and doing this inner work. They teach this to help you bridge the gap and bring you back to higher consciousness. That is how you heal your electromagnetic grid and the divine feminine.

How many of you have seen the movie Dr. Strange? For those of you who haven't, I highly recommend it. The way the movie visually depicts travel in the astral realm is a perfect representation of my personal experience of astral travel. If I had to give someone a visual of what astral travel is like, that would be it! In the scene where Dr. Strange meets the Ancient One, she tells him, "I know how to reorient the spirit to better heal the body." He then says with sarcasm, "You are talking to me about healing through belief!? All right, how do we do that? Where do we start?" She then shows him images in a book of MRI scans, acupuncture points, and a chiropractic chart. Things go a bit sideways from there as Dr. Strange grows frustrated with the ridiculousness of her notion that we can find the answer to instantaneous physical healing in those charts. He is after all a brilliant doctor. What I would like to focus on is what the Ancient One says right after. She says, "Each of those maps was drawn up by someone who could see in part, but not the whole."

We are now working toward remembering the parts as a whole. The truth is your biology has never just consisted of your mind, body, and soul. You were made of other amazing and wondrous facets. Source consciousness intended for you to experience reality fully connecting to the frequency of Source. Your spirit and physical body were created in his image. Energy. That is why in this time of the Golden Age, many of us are awaking to the desire to connect back to the body, heal the body, live and thrive in the body. In order to experience the life Source Consciousness intended for us to experience, it is important to begin to understand our electromagnetic technology, heal our past, heal the divine feminine, and do the inner work.

ARIANE OATES

ARIANE OATES IS CONNECTED to the Alpha and Omega – the beginning and the end.

Her journey with the inner alchemy required to synthesize conscious and unconscious multi-dimensional fragments, and aspects of self, via the depths of her inner and higher heart process, have been aligned with the group body of Energetic Synthesis, founded by Lisa Renee.

She is of the Grandmother Turtle lineage and holds the Turtle Shield #11 in the collection, that was created by a Norther American Shaman. Grandmother Turtle Codes have been protected, embodied and hidden, by the aboriginal and indigenous cultures of the earth for eons of time.

Ariane is well versed in the Law of One/The Law of Love – which is the heroic journey home to full embodiment is an inner heart expansion.

The law of one are the natural laws governing universal creation with the understanding that all One is the recognition of Eternal Truth is Eternal Love and Eternal Love is organic consciousness of infinite creator. This translates into the Eternal God like human who leads the way for others.

Ariane holds the field of pure creation through her Source Connection, and offers personal sessions to those on an advanced level. These sessions facilitate an immediate acceleration of consciousness.

Here is how to find out more about Ariane Oates:

https://www.facebook.com/ArianeOatesWisdomPeaces

THE SACRED LANGUAGE OF NUMBERS

BY ARIANE OATES

THE WORD MATHEMA – *signified "learning in general" and as the root of the Old English mathein, "to be aware" and the old German munthen, "to awaken". Ancients saw numbers and shapes as symbols to explain the divine and organic structure of human nature, the dance of the cosmos and communion with God Source Intelligence.*

Consciousness speaks many languages underneath the guise of third dimensional reality. Not all of Her dialects are linguistic.

Many are subtle, energetic whispers—nuances that evoke awakening and awareness. When we are consciously seeking greater meaning, something breaks through the ordinariness of our lives and wakes us up.

Initially, I gathered information as a dream walker, moving through earth, within the elegant beauty of my dream come true life. I knew there were other worlds elsewhere, everywhere, that were overlays to my human experience. One day I woke up to energies under the 3D narrative. I didn't even have to peek beyond the matrix, as subtexts flashed through like neon lights. When the alarm clock of your awakening rings, at 22 minutes past 2 you see the meaning in and behind All Things. I started to awaken within the dreams I was walking yet became aware of other dreams and different worlds that higher aspects of My Self resided within. I started to perceive the dialects of color, energy, the spirit world, syncronicity and numerical sequences. And through these sub-texts I realized all were deeper communications of consciousness and spoke languages that were long forgotten in the 3D narrative.

Most of us come to Earth with greater purposes and higher missions that often extend beyond the conceptualization of our logical mind. I am a cosmic calculator and a number gnostic. I see the language of numbers, integrate these into my body and facilitate the higher meanings into the 3 d reality and Earth plane; as a new language for humanity that spans multi-dimensions of time.

There is a divine infinite calculus that is it uttered from the cosmic heart of the Holy Mother. This articulates God's mathematical creation sequences—sacred geometrical structures that are the spine of everything in on earth and within the cosmos.

There are codes in words and nature; in art and music. Algorithms formulas, birth dates, addresses, bank account numbers, phone numbers, the latitude and longitude of geographic local: the list goes on and on. My body and being perceive and receive these as if they are intonations activating my God Essence. I connect these communications through observation, understanding and vocalized expression so that they can expand into the collective consciousness.

The higher energetic resonance of the number sequence alters our perception, which then expands our experience. Our awareness elevates and we look behind the walls of 3d reality and see something more. Lightening higher densities of energy; a higher meaning, a confirmation, a message is whispered.

When our awakened consciousness is fully present and embodied in the now moment, the energy that seeds our thought and expression imprints or catalyzes vibrations that transform reality. The words we speak for our potently awakened state can now activate reality.

Heart rules over the mind. Through heart resonance—we see, hear and feel the words within words—and the language within numbers.

Numbers are energetic codes that speak their language through the nuances of the realities they communicate and activate. They can access multiple layers of consciousness and other lifetimes if you allow yourself to open up energetically and receive their frequencies. Often what is streaming through via the ever increasing upgrades of cosmic light also ends of defining what are the details behind the number codes and their communication and activation to and through you. Because number sequences are part of God's communication to you, they end up opening you to your own God essence too. Those of us who are particularly drawn to the language of numbers are time keepers of these codes. Our light bodies have calculation sequences which unravel and decode these hidden energies when synthesizing new streams of cosmic frequency.

There are feelings and energies behind these numerical sequences and as we witness these, the sequences are recoded and reencrypted into new fields of energy. Sometimes they are calculation sequences that activate our light body. When we integrate the omnidimensional energies behind number sequences our slumbering God Source Intelligence begins to awaken.

There is a conscious cryptography whispering the symbolic of Divinely inspired expression. If we don't perceive, witness, receive and physically actualize the communication/transformation of the numerical sequence, it does not grace us with God's whisper and we don't up level our vibration. What you be and do becomes a creation that extends beyond you and your life and contributes to collective change.

Our awareness and embodiment of our divinity brings us into communion with Source Intelligence. Through this unity, we are continuously in communication with God. As Source Intelligence merges with everything—through the rapid evolution of consciousness, new languages and vibrations surface. There are transformative and telepathic nuances within number coded information packets. But One must open to perceiving and receiving these Creator communications.

Each being holds and communicates frequencies wherever they are on the Earth. Their birth date and the lineage they carry hold numerical frequencies which, when combined with the date and time and latitude and longitude of where they are experiencing, they are vibrationally upgraded and align with a new, higher reality creation.

Everything has to be witnessed and physicalized in order for it to complete into creation. Physicalization is an act of non-judgment and no attachment. It is a neutral process that integrates the polarities of positive and negative in the receiving process of it. Because it's neutral, it allows for higher vibrational energies to flow into our direct experience. These cosmic frequencies streams are threads of stories within the greater narrative of our Ascension timeline. Embodiment is physicalization. Everything around you is part of your universe. Your Inner and outer experiences Become One template energy form just by being and receiving all the Oneness is communicating within and outside of you.

As you look beyond the initial impression of any number sequence, you deconstruct language and reality to get to the truth. Everything is speaking to you as you go out into the world and live your daily life. Are you willing to receive it?

Just as a weaver creates a tapestry what you witness, perceive and embody is braided or woven into the alignment of your higher being when you are awake enough to hold it. There are always subtexts of a Divine human factor being woven in with the warp and weft of number sequences. We live within a hologram that is continually altered by new cosmic frequencies. The numerical codes that are within our hologram are an abacus that continuously calculates the transformational potential of these frequencies upgrading our beingness.

How can the sacred language of numbers contribute your consciousness expansion?

- When you awaken to number codes appearing in your life, your perspective shifts and you become aware of things you never saw before.

- Because number codes have unique energetic fields with blueprints of their own, and a consciousness communication of their own, learning their language inspires higher awareness. Through witnessing, acknowledging and receiving the elevated energy of numbers, you bring the energy of higher consciousness into the earth plane.

- Numerical symbols catalyze new energetic patterns that are required for your consciousness expansion.

- When numerical sequences show up in your experiences and you witness them—their vibration transmits through your body.

- When we notice and embody the energies of number codes we override unconsciousness. We recover memories of other timelines and energetic frequencies.

- 222, 444, 999 and other numbers in triplicate are Master numbers and deliberately arranged to awaken your consciousness and activate your personal blueprint. This means you start to shift perspective and become more aware of things you not previously aware of.

- Like a mathematical equation where $3+33=9$, number codes are an orchestration of events that line up with the highest probable outcome.

- The physical action of what you are doing is a creation in and of itself. When a number code becomes visible during the act of creation there is an additional frequency and that contributes to a new refined creation

- Some sequences can activate dormant memories from other higher dimensional existences and fields of energy inspiring DNA re-encryption and activation

- Numbers are connection sequences that support the energetic building blocks of Christ Consciousness.

- The higher energetic resonance of the number sequence alters our perception, which then expands our experience. Our awareness elevates and we look behind the walls of 3d reality and see something more. Lightening higher densities of energy; a higher meaning, a confirmation, a message is whispered.

- When our awakened consciousness is fully present and embodied in the now moment, the energy that seeds our thought and expression imprints or catalyzes vibrations that transforms reality. The words we speak for our potently awakened state can now activate reality.

How to understand the language of numbers:

- Intend to bring your full presence into embodiment in your now moment. This way you can open up a gateway into direct communication with your Avatar Self and the higher spiritual realm.

- Most people start to awaken to the nuances of number language when seeing number sequences on clocks, watches, cell phones and other technology. Then license plates, bank accounts, addresses begin to offer energetic resonances which draw your attention. Make note of repeating number sequences that show up as you become aware of what you are doing in the Now Moment. This will provide you with deeper meaning within the number subtext that is uttered from your guidance or higher consciousness. Certain associations with a particular number can trace or weave a higher story.

- Just as an alarm clock wakes you up at a particular time you set it... a number sequence rings your awareness to another level of Awakening. Don't collapse into ordinary thought but perceive everything energetically in the Now Moment. What are you sensing? What were you experiencing? What were you thinking? Receive the energy of all this and make notes of all that is showing up. Is your energy and consciousness transforming as you expand into receiving all the nuances of your now moment? If so in what direction? Commune directly with the energy of the number sequence. Asks its consciousness what message it has or you.

- Because each being is unique, the message behind the number code is your interpretation and no one else's. The numerical arrangements within your astrological chart influence the communicated code significances. There is no right or wrong way to interpret and number code. Chances are your code message will differ from what is "spoken" to someone else.

- Analyze the number codes in your birth date. These will often compliment the number codes that show up in your life, offering a more specific meaning when these show up. Each letter of your name also has a numerical equivalent. Adding these numbers together can show you your life path or higher purpose. Explore the birth dates of your family members, close friends and pets: and other significant dates like marriages or deaths to discover the numerical blueprint that contributes to your spiritual evolution. Every being that is within the fabric of our lives contributes to our life story. Through discovering the deeper communication offered through numerical codes, we can find answers to our own personal journey.

- Begin by asking your Source Self: What questions can I ask here that will enable me to find the higher significance behind this particular number sequence at this particular time. What are the questions you can ask when a particular number sequence shows up you can? Are you already in the process of clearing another timeline based on the cosmic alignments and frequency upgrades? Are there lessons you are learning from close people in your life? Is story lines you need to complete?

What do you need to forgive and release? What is your higher purpose? What do you need to be aware of to develop greater mastery?

- Be aware of the time that these numerical symbols show up. Because time is measured numerically, it contributes a subplot to the energetic activation.

Stepping into the universal language of numbers invites you to connect with the original language of God. The foundational structure behind everything on earth and in the cosmos sings these celestial tones of infinite beingness. Being aware of geometry behind all things enables you to transcend time and the 3 dimensional construct of reality. Numerical codes create a particular connection to you based on your unique universe providing profound initiation and greater meaning to your spiritual evolution.

LAURA EISENHOWER

LAURA EISENHOWER IS A Global Alchemist, Researcher and Medical and Intuitive Astrologist. She is an internationally acclaimed speaker who has presented her work worldwide. Laura is the great-granddaughter of President Dwight David Eisenhower, and she reveals Exopolitical information about his administration that has been largely held in secrecy. Many consider her to be one of North Americas leading researchers on: Health, Exopolitics, Alchemy, Metaphysics, and Galactic History. Laura works to free us from the 3-D holographic time-loop, False Archonic systems and Military Industrial Complex. She exposes hidden agendas to foster human sovereignty. Feeling a calling regarding her mission since she was a child, she gained incredible insight through her wilderness adventures and psychic development. She connects major dots to guide humanity into higher Earth energies. Laura has a deep understanding of Gaia-Sophia and our Divine Blueprint and how they connect to the Venus transits, Earth grids, Global Alchemy, DNA & ET races. Her passion is to inspire Unity Consciousness and bring us back to the Zero point/Unified field—the totality of our divine powers.

How to find more about Laura Eisenhower:

Her website is https://cosmicgaia.org/
https://www.youtube.com/user/LauraEisenhower
https://www.facebook.com/groups/1057954054381456/
https://twitter.com/LauraMagdalene4

Awaken to the Bigger Picture:
Your Choices and Actions Create a New Earth

BY LAURA EISENHOWER

Because of soul agreements, I incarnated into the Eisenhower bloodline in this lifetime. I also made sure that I would embark on a journey that would help me understand this Mother Earth intimately. I developed a deep connection with Her and discovered a great galactic love story that lives in our DNA and the soul of this planet.

The Magdalene flame, that I and many women carry, would weave in with the Eisenhower family energies. This tapestry became the foundation of a mission that is all about this paradigm shift and time of awakening. Because our shadow governments intentionally targeted the Earth and the Divine Feminine and Masculine, Eisenhower and I share in a legacy of Disclosure which wasn't achievable in his era. He has always been a Spirit guide to me.

The return of love and reverence to our Mother Earth and the fundamental nature of Unity Consciousness is rising, as we recognize the manipulations and dark technologies that have stunted our growth.

Though I felt the immensity of this family connection, synchronicities lead me to many psychics, channels and clairvoyants who helped me to see and understand the cosmic connection I have with my great grandfather. I came to Earth through this family lineage to help bring awareness to things held in secrecy and also to reveal our greater Galactic history and human potential. I am on earth as a Guardian of the Organic Ascension timeline, here as a catalyst for Global Alchemy to repair and restore human DNA and Earth grids and to assist us in discovering our multi-dimensional Nature and full Spectrum of Vibrational Frequency.

My great-grandfather, Dwight D. Eisenhower, led the Allied Forces to victory over Hitler before being elected the 34th President of the United States of America. In office, he kept the peace for eight years. During this time, something else was building underneath the surface, beyond his control: connections to extraterrestrials, hidden agendas involving Mars, Secret Space programs and a global elitist dark Cabal and their many projects. I heavily researched ET government treaties and visitations from different groups of beings to discover some answers. These Dark Forces penetrated much of what he worked hard to create. In a famous speech, Ike warned;

"In the councils of government, we must guard against the acquisition of unwarranted influence, whether sought or unsought, by the Military–Industrial Complex. The potential for the disastrous rise of misplaced power exists and will persist. We must never let the weight of this combination endanger our liberties or democratic processes. We should take nothing for granted. Only an alert and knowledgeable citizenry can compel the proper meshing of the huge industrial and military machinery of defense with our peaceful methods and goals so that security and liberty may prosper together."

I discovered that my path would take me right into the heart of what Great Grandfather was talking about. His warning about the Military Industrial Complex gives insight to this growing misplaced power that infiltrated all sectors of our military, government and society. The weapons industry started as a small group of wealthy and powerful people who sought to profit from war. They threatened democracy and peace in the world.

I have always felt my great grandfather's presence and guidance with me. We both were born with soul missions, and the goals of these missions are similar. We are both Libras, seekers of balance and justice. Many who wish for another agenda to overtake this planet have distorted and targeted both of our true intentions.

There are Dark Forces at play on earth, many of them alien: ET races have always been interacting with this planet. Some have a hidden agenda to keep humanity unconscious and locked into a time loop. Others are benevolent. Because of our multi-dimensional nature we are connected to them. They are part of a greater Galactic heritage to discover.

There is a NET placed around this Earth and seals placed in our DNA to make it very difficult to expand into higher energies. This is the result of some controller groups and a need to be quarantined. These controlling factions have fought many wars regarding how to handle humanity. Many dismiss claims like this as conspiracy theories. However, in the many years I have done events and astrological readings, I have met countless individuals who have been contacted by ET groups. Many of these people were abducted and pushed into breeding programs. Others were survivors of human-trafficking, Satanic Ritual Abuse and pedophilia. The Controllers responsible for these atrocities still hold power. They are behind The New World Order, fake media and false narratives pushed onto humanity through false flag events and psychological operations.

Humanity is not the only life form in the cosmos. There are many competing agendas on Earth. People within these power structures and those with certain bloodlines consider us a harvestable food source necessary to maintain their power. Kept in the dark for so long about so much, we have come to accept ourselves as a limited human form. Mind-control, social conditioning and indoctrination have made it very difficult to remember who we truly are and what our potential is.

We are part of a Galactic History filled with War and what we see occurring on Earth now results from hidden shadow elements and elite bloodlines acting as Dark Over Lords. Mainstream society controls and compartmentalizes outer information deliberately to target our anxieties and fears. We need to stop propaganda, release others' projections and refuse to buy into the dangerous narratives dictating what our future will be.

Step back and look objectively at the larger picture with an open mind. Begin to refine it down to something that works with us and for us, rather than against us. Our creative imagination, willpower and leadership need to expand. We need to speak up and call out the crimes against humanity. Human advancement needs to come with a greater respect for this Earth and a greater understanding of the abundance of herbs and medicines that it holds. Transhumanism and AI are not human advancement. They DESTROY our Soul and DNA and are a false solution to the World's problems. Because these problems are purposely induced, it is of great importance that we understand who the actual enemies are and not turn on one another.

Many of us came to earth to recover the Fall of Humankind. Others are here to bring about Disclosure and clear inorganic entities from Stargates; do grid work and help birth Unity Consciousness and assist humanity evolving into Higher Earth energies.

This is a time where we as a human race are being tasked with awakening to our true potential, deeper origins, and our connection to this Planet and Cosmos. To get to the Truth, this task requires us to dig deep and go way outside of our comfort zone. We must let go of what we thought was reality and much of what we were taught.

True liberation of humanity is only possible when we do the inner work, seek self-knowledge and live by higher principles like integrity and compassion. We must avoid getting locked into a trajectory and false Timelines engineered and imposed upon us. If we can't see our own true organic Nature and relationship with Cosmic and Natural law, we buy into fear generating false realities. Then we comply, consent, and give our power away even more as we become desperate for a solution.

Ascension is the blossoming of human consciousness and the anchoring of the Mother energies back into the Earth body. It is our expansion into other dimensions and the activation of dormant DNA. This enables grid repair and catalyzes the transformation of our bodies from a carbon base to a crystalline, silicate matrix. The Silicate Matrix is the Original Human blueprint designed to manifest 12 strings of DNA and beyond. This embodied expression allows humans to travel inter-dimensionally and exist without deterioration of the biological form.

In the manipulated Artificial Timeline World, there are super computer systems that sends waves of desires out at just the right moment to influence the masses. These are coordinated with the media, scalar and weather events, and natural biological cycles. When we are on the precipice of an evolutionary leap, the negative forces always create something to hi-jack it. We need to gain a greater understanding of Dark technologies and discover ways we can protect ourselves. We have to gain ownership over our minds and move into the vibration of Love and Wisdom and understand the Diamond Heart activations of the Earth.

Everything is mapped out by an artificial intelligence system designed to prohibit humanity from awareness of their true power. This is something we have to override.

There is an artificial Matrix which is a construct based on imitation of the organic World. The Gaia Matrix exists as the true foundation with an Archontic AI overlay that puts things in reversals. We digress instead of advance as a race. The Organic timeline is habitable through authenticity, internal freedom and Natural World connection. We are an advanced technology and our DNA can upgrade and reveal this. The AI false reality, simulates and imitates things in distorted ways. When we fall into conflict and confusion and we are being defined by external forces, we are more easily controlled. At a time where we need to embrace Unity Consciousness, we are being pulled back into race wars and the shame, blame and guilt game.

The choices we make and where we align our energies, are detrimental to creating our future. We need to keep our creative channels clear and not allow infection by what's streaming in through the television and devices. Rediscovering our genuine divine nature is fundamental as it inspires the bravery required to transcend social programming and AI timelines. Truth stands on its own and it will exist whether or not we find it, same with Spirit. Truth has a resonance with our physical bodies and heals and regenerates us. Falsities cause damage: belief systems put upon us create health issues. Understanding the roots of our afflictions, and hearing the messages of wisdom that live in our intuition and higher mind, create transformation. Higher dimensional awareness must be integrated into the physical plane for us to see a change for the better.

Main stream society programs humanity to exist at a very basic ego level. Targeting disconnects our minds and our divine creative power: we don't seek true liberation and instead become the product of some other self-serving agenda. We are tricked into this and encouraged to stay in the lower levels so self, which include false ego gratification, suffering and hopelessness. If we stay soul centered, our ego nature can fully merge with our true identity and multi-dimensional nature.

Our DNA is made up of elements of nature and connects with Earth grids. We are powerful co-creators with this Earth. Cosmic alignments, with the stars and the Sun moving into the 13th sign, and the great conjunctions happening, show that transformation is occurring encoded in us, the Earth and stars. Called the Stellar Activation Cycle, the ancients were aware of how important this window of time is, connected with the Venus transits and the opening of Stargates.

Our opportunity to transform and reclaim our lost aspects is at a peak period, the end of an approximately 26,000 year cycle connected to the Procession of the Equinoxes. Natural forces know how to activate and advance us. We need to create space for this and not take the human realm too personally.

This World was once far less dense than it is today. When we dealt with Galactic Wars, cataclysms and the collapse of the higher dimensional civilizations, caused by exploding planets, that rapidly changed. We experienced violation of free will and hybridization and the manipulation of incarnate consciousness, and our DNA.

We are all fragmented. We are born with amnesia about the past. Being raised into society often means indoctrination into something that lures us into many traps. If we fall prey to these, we may struggle with self-worth issues and insecurities. There is so much unresolved trauma we carry and are unconscious of. New traumas are inflicted. We need to rid the World of these destructive, power-hungry people and learn how these bloodlines of the Cabal operate.

Awakening is about waking up to who we truly are. This enables us to view reality in other ways. Our own advanced consciousness is energetically possible to attain on Earth, and we need to dedicate ourselves to finding it.

We all have our own unique roles. When you ask yourself, what is your purpose or mission, it will reveal itself in your everyday life and in dream time. Looking at your passions and your wounds is a good place to start. Oneness is diversity in harmony.

We must be comfortable experiencing all of our inner elements: Earth, Air, Fire, Water, Aether. Once we purify ourselves of negative patterns, we can connect with Cosmic and Earthly forces in Oneness. This is about alignment with Source Intelligence. Sovereignty means you are no longer enslaved in your mind or in your life. You can find integrity, internal harmony and the creative imagination working with Cosmic and Natural law, to help us correct ourselves, heal and find a true balance with those around us. Oneness is diversity in harmony.

Our deeper intuition is often overshadowed by belief systems. Our greatest hopes and fears are targeted: we stay lost because we aren't operating from our own insights and Truth. We need to get to the core roots of our origins, discover what our DNA is really about, and what harms us and heals us, so we can develop healthy boundaries. We heal when we are in touch with our own passions and inspirations and can recognize the source of our pain and wounds.

Facing the Dark Night of the Soul initiations are unavoidable. It can be very confusing for some to begin to connect with their depths. The sensation of dying is part of this process. It can put one in a panic and create a lot of stress, but if we can let go a bit, the organic Alchemy and transformation can work its magic. This paradigm shift is about letting go of the old system and allowing that death within ourselves, so we can rise in our greatness. The old system, the re-writing of history, the distortions of the masculine and feminine and social engineering, are things that need to go. Planetary conjunctions are encouraging this with Pluto, Saturn and Jupiter.

It is important that humanity advances spiritually, in balance with technology. It is a shift from the inside out and an initiation. The Earth responds to us.

When we see the options for our future that are based in our dreams, goals and visions, we expand and see more of ourselves and discover more choices than we may have thought possible. We are Artists of Energy that keep pushing the envelope; constantly nudged by greater forces into an unfolding divine blueprint, like a rose bud beginning to blossom. We are not at the mercy of the surrounding reality. We can work with it and change it. When we transform, so does our reality. That doesn't mean we don't witness other future scenarios that others are choosing. We will see a vast contrast, rather than fear that we might be subjected to going down the same road.

In order to evolve we must integrate polarity. We have more than five senses to experience and integrate. We have higher strand DNA and Galactic Chakras that hold the Sacred Union energies. These reveal the greater Love story we are all a part of. Imbalance keeps us stuck, and it attracts dark entities. Our darkness is the womb that receives seeds from our higher mind, to create and generate a beautiful reality if we allow it. If we don't work on energetic hygiene and maintenance, things overtake the aspects of ourselves we are trying to nurture and grow.

If we draw in seeds from our fears and haunted imagination, we enable the existence of the very things we want to stop. We have to come face to face with fear, learning to triumph over it. We are undefeatable if we keep reaching for more. We have the infinite to reach into. We need to surrender more to the love story that exists in our DNA and recognize the Divinity in Nature and Cosmos and let that flow into us and from us.

Every part of us requires maintenance or things get toxic and out of balance. Internalized emotions and too much on the mind can attract the same things that a sink full of dirty dishes would. Heart-ache without tears or release, can create pain and lower the immune system. Any form of repression or accumulation creates issues. It's obvious when things need clearing in the physical World. Depression is apparent, but solutions from society are dangerous: as are the coping mechanisms or ways one masks what they are feeling. Pain needs a voice. One needs to understand their dissatisfaction and then make it a mission to heal it, solve it, or bring attention to it.

Being plugged into anything other than Love, our higher wisdom and Spirit, can be dangerous. We need to make a daily practice of staying connected, working on our shadow and going deeper into our unconsciousness. Bringing this into consciousness will connect us with more creative power and options. We hold an override frequency when we stay connected to our core Nature and our creations are stronger than the false matrix.

One of my main goals is to connect many dots, so we can integrate fragments and see a fuller picture that isn't so compartmentalized. We are very much the World we see around us and the conditions of our own self are amplified in the outer World. We receive it back to us as a reality we sometimes create fixed beliefs about: it stares us in the face so that we do something, not so that we submit to it and further digress. We are taught to do the opposite of what Natural and Cosmic Laws encourage us to do. When we have opportunities to advance, many freak out and get more and more entangled in the control mechanisms that siphon our life force. Advancement isn't pain free. Most run from pain or want a quick fix cure, rather than take the time to learn from it. Healing brings us closer to ourselves rather than further away. We need to allow adversity to bless us with greater self-knowledge, rather than fear and disconnect from self.

There is no such thing as total human enslavement unless you give up your connection with your Soul and alignment with Spirit and Earth. We are on a journey within the fields of the creative imagination. This can get haunted and compromised into beliefs that help to enable the end times propaganda and manifestation of things we may not wish to create. If our creative channels hold our own divine instructions, we collapse Timelines and walk in authentic freedom. It is just a matter of time for the physical to catch up with a shift in consciousness.

If fear shows up, it can open a doorway into Truth if you will kick the door down and not submit to the concept of being trapped. It is only within ourselves we become trapped; through limiting our beliefs about what is possible. There are always tools, shields, magic and keys: if something pushes against us, our determination can push back and then break through.

This is a time where it is critical we wake up. It is our true Divinity and treasures we are re-discovering. In finding this, we find like-minded people and Soul family and we help plant seeds in others. We give others permission to become their true authentic self and we detach from the things that keep us stuck and hold us back. This is true leadership, being your authentic self. Let yourself take this leap. Seek your greatest potential and embody it. Know you are not alone!

KAISA ROSE

KAISA ROSE STRIVES TO bring harmony and understanding to the lives of those she works with. She offers readings, energetic healing, and counseling to her clients. Her goal is to help people transform their lives and develop healthier relationships with themselves and others.

You can find out more about Kaisa here:

Her website: www.itskaisarose.com
www.facebook.com/itskaisarose
www.twitter.com/itskaisarose
or via email itskaisarose@gmail.com

The Awakening of an Arcturian Starseed

BY KAISA ROSE

My name is Kaisa Rose and I am an Arcturian Starseed and Ascension Guide. A Starseed is a soul that has chosen to incarnate into a human life on Earth, bringing with them the knowledge and abilities of higher dimensional beings in order to assist the planet and humanity with awakening. I am here to help awaken other Starseed souls through connecting them to the Starseed identity. In this chapter I will describe the traits of a Starseed, share my personal experience with awakening, and give advice to those seeking their identity.

The Starseed mission is what sets us apart from other souls. We incarnate with information, knowledge, and abilities that will aid Earth and its people in raising their vibration. In order to access or unlock that information we must awaken ourselves. Once we have moved through our spiritual awakening, we connect with the Starseed identity and begin our path of ascension. It is this path which leads us to our purpose in life. Similar to an indigo child, a Starseed is a term to categorize souls with a certain energetic mission. We have a strong connection to our Starseed origins and may have memories of those places. Starseed origins are important in our awakening process as we are assisted and comforted by connecting with the galaxies and star systems we have come from. Some of these Starseed origins include Andromeda, Orion, Arcturus, Lyra, Sirius, and Pleiades. There are many more than just the ones I have listed. You may connect with more than one race of inter dimensional being and those beings could occupy more than one location. It is quite possible to connect with different origins and beings at different points in your ascension process. I first connected with Orion. Then I was deeply connected to Andromeda until I was of a high enough vibration to connect with Arcturus. These energies all serve to assist you and your mission. When connecting with them, allow yourself to explore and connect with whatever serves you best at the time.

How do you know you're a Starseed? Typically, Starseeds have a difficult childhood and may experience abuse and trauma early in life. These circumstances serve to push us to personal growth at a faster rate through seeking self-healing, thus accelerating the awakening process. Because we must awaken to unlock our abilities and fulfill our purpose on this planet, we have a fast track on the awakening process. But this fast track is full of hardships that create discomfort pushing us toward positive change and growth. You may feel alienated in social settings and like you never fit into society. You could feel that no one ever truly understands you and you may struggle to understand your own place in the mainstream world. Another common trait is a history of sinus issues and sensitivities to food and medicines. Often natural remedies and Eastern medicine work best for your body and Western medicine may cause more harm than good. You may communicate with spirit guides or your higher self. Do you have vivid dreams of other realities and lives? Do you identify as an empath? These are traits of a Starseed. If any of this resonates with you, you likely are a Starseed! If you do not feel you are a Starseed, you still have a beautiful purpose on this planet. A Starseed is just one role a soul may have on this planet. You may now be able to recognize Starseeds in your life and connect with them in a new way!

I'll explain how I came to awaken to the Starseed identity. My Starseed awakening came around the age of 21. The first twenty years of my life were very traumatic. I wanted to break free of the abusive patterns in my life and become a better person. I no longer wanted to be a victim. So, I set the intention of self-discovery and healing. I wanted to become someone new that was capable of a healthier way of living.

One night, out of nowhere, the word Starseed was planted into my mind. I kept hearing "Starseed" replay over and over again in my brain. I took to the internet! Searching for a meaning behind this term, I found many articles that presented what the word meant and then had a questionnaire for people to see if you identify as a Starseed. The descriptions and natural abilities that characterized a Starseed resonated so deeply with me. My soul felt like it was being reunited with a long-lost identity. I felt validation for feeling different my whole life. This new identity of a Starseed was taking root in my heart and encouraged me to grow spiritually in search of more answers.

My Catholic upbringing taught me that we have this one human life and when we die there is no rebirth. You end up in heaven or hell for the rest of eternity. This always felt so limiting. The idea of one life never felt satisfying. I was always curious about other religions and philosophies. Reincarnation always fascinated me. Past lives were so intriguing. When I connected with the Starseed identity, everything seemed to finally make sense. Of course, we could have an eternal soul that has experienced many different dimensions of being. The universe is far older than our planet. It made sense that my soul would have taken form on other planets or in other galaxies before coming to this Earth.

Here was where my ego came into play. Some of the articles I read talked about how rare a Starseed soul was. I interpreted that as the rest of humanity having human souls that had never experienced anything outside of this planet. I distanced myself from humanity in this way. It made me feel special to think that I was a rare being. In this way, I did not have to identify as human and all the baggage that comes along with that. At the time, being human depressed me. I could only see the negative aspects of our collective humanity. No longer identifying as a human was a huge release of the shame that I felt about how people treat one another and this planet. As well as the guilt I felt about my role in the negativity I had observed and experienced thus far in my life.

As I read more, I came to realize that every soul on Earth was connected to mine. Even if someone is not on the Starseed mission, our souls originate from the same source energy. In that, we are all connected, and our souls originate from a higher plane of existence. Again, this is where I noticed my ego. It was reaffirming this idea of being a rare gift to the Earth. Like I was an alien princess incarnate. So, as I searched for more information, I started to find things that challenged my ego. For example, the Higher Self. The belief that our souls are all higher energetic life forms that, in the Earth's case, take the form of humans to further their development or help with what is going on with the planet. This higher energy form that we are connected to is the Higher Self. So, if we all have a Higher Self, then no one is simply a human living one human life and forever ceasing to exist upon their human death. While all souls may not be defined as Starseeds, all souls are connected more so than I originally assumed.

My ego did not want to let go of this distance I had created between myself and humanity. My spiritual growth would have halted there if I had caved to the denial. Ego can trap us and prevent growth by redirecting our focus to negative thinking. As quickly as I had distanced myself from the human race, I was right back in the collective. I felt disgusted at this notion of being like the rest of humanity. My ego was clinging to this brief belief that I was special, superior even. So, what was I to do? Do I deny this truth that I had found just to satisfy my vanity? If I had chosen to side with my ego, I would have disconnected myself from my truth. Without overcoming my selfish subconscious, my learning and growth would have come to a halt. Instead I surrendered to being connected to all souls. There was fear that I would lose pieces of my identity that made me unique but that is change. Isn't it? We must let the old fall away to make room for the new. I am so glad that I did.

Setting out on your spiritual journey of discovery, it is important to keep moving. Imagine your journey much like exploring a museum. You want to move through all the rooms to have a balanced experience. A man who stays in only one section will have a skewed life.

There are so many amazing things on and off this planet. For me, I was wrapped up in exploring my past lives. Past lives and knowing the future fascinated me. I wanted to know so much about both my past and my future, but I did not want to focus on my present. After pursuit of these topics no longer served me, I came to see these as distractions. There is nothing wrong with wanting to know more about past lives or what the future may hold but I was focusing on them as a form of escape from the inner work that needed to be done in my present.

This is a caution to losing yourself to mental escapism. The same can be said for UFOs. Some people make it their life's work to shed light on the subject and witness them. There is nothing inherently wrong with that. My concern comes from the people I see who are wrapped up in the idea of an Extra-Terrestrial race rescuing them or bringing change to life as we know it. We should not look outside of ourselves and our human race for solutions to our problems. Our personal growth can be aided by others, but it is our responsibility to heal. It is easy to shift blame and responsibility onto others. We give our power away by doing that.

This is one of my biggest pieces of advice. Do not get caught up in obsession. Keep a balance between human experience and spiritual growth. It can be easy to become fixated on a particular subject. You want to be sure that you don't fall into a mindset where anyone or anything is rescuing you from the unhappiness in your life. Happiness or ease is achieved through doing the personal work and learning how to create a happier life for yourself. As Starseeds, we have a lot of inner work to do, usually in a short period, to get us up to speed so that we may positively influence the earth. The key is: We must do the work. You have the power to transform your life in every single aspect. Focus on how you can provide that for yourself instead of getting hung up on something else giving it to you.

You probably have a lot of questions about how to proceed down this path. I know I did. I sought out intuits, readers, and healers to aid in my self-discovery. It's very important to understand how to discern what is in alignment for your highest good. There are negative beings and forces that make it their mission to interfere and stop the ascension of Starseeds. This is because a single Starseed is capable of creating an energetic ripple effect that raises the vibration of the planet, places, and people around them just by existing. Your vibration or frequency is the energetic signature you carry. The more inner work you do, the higher your vibration can rise. The more your vibration rises, the more abilities or senses will come online, and you will start experiencing life in new ways. Negative beings may try to frighten you off or keep you stuck in one place. Finding mentors is important not just for your own growth but to develop a sense of community. It can be lonely feeling like an alien in a human body!

Seeking mentors can be a frustrating process. Trust your instincts. When you find the right person, you will know without a doubt in your mind! Never doubt yourself or try to force a situation to feel right. That was something I often found myself doing, trying to take a person, place, or thing, and fit it into my idea of how my life should be. I was doing this out of fear that I would never be worthy of finding what I truly desired. This goes hand in hand with manifestation. We cannot put manifestation into practice when we do not feel worthy. Sure, we may want a better job or financial abundance, but if we are afraid of having those things, we will always block our ability to manifest them.

Healing the scarcity mindset was vital for me. I always wanted more but I did not feel worthy or capable of having it. This all stemmed from a lack of self-worth. Through healing those issues, I was able to step into my power. My final piece of advice is to practice energetic hygiene. I was always seeking energy healing when I was in a crisis. I knew how to protect myself. I knew how to clean my energy field, but I was simply not doing it until I was in a bad spot. Once I started taking that more seriously, I came online to my abilities within weeks. I realized that by creating a healthier energetic space, I was allowing energetic downloads and upgrades to take place. This allowed me to step into my Starseed identity in a way that allows me to help others.

If you resonate with the Starseed Identity, then know that you are fully supported and have a place and purpose on this planet! Through connecting with your Starseed identity, you will be able to grow spiritually and unlock your gifts and life's purpose. I hope you enjoy your journey and embrace your purpose on this planet!

SHIRLEY BARBOUR

SHIRLEY BARBOUR IS A Creativity Coach, Writer and Spirit Communicator. She connects with ease to the Spirit world and to those that have passed. She is a bestselling author in another Anthology, The Energy of Spirit. Shirley is an inspirational and creative writer that inspires her readers with her authentic writing style. In 2021 she will have two books published.

Shirley has been creative all her life and some of her creative pursuits have been in art, painting, drawing, sewing, crafts and writing. She also has a thirst for knowledge with interests in numerology, reflexology, iridology and aromatherapy.

In Shirley's life, any time she was ready to give up, she pulled herself up by the bootstraps and forged her way through. To do this, she had to embrace places she did not want to go. She follows the lightness in her daily endeavors to create the future that is waiting for her. Shirley is a guiding force for people to follow that are struggling to put one foot in front of the other and to know which direction to go next.

With her gentle manner and caring nature, she offers others the space to step into more of themselves. Laughter and joy are an intrinsic part of who she is.

There have been many modalities, courses and books that have expanded her awareness. Personal Best Seminars, Warrior Sage, Access Consciousness and Julie Renee Doering and books by Satyen Raja, Doreen Virtue, Gary Zukav, Gary Douglas and Dr. Dain Heer.

How to find out more about Shirley Barbour:

Her website is www.shirleybarbour.com
You can reach out to her by email at shirlf@shaw.ca

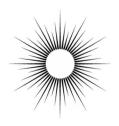

How to Connect To Spirit Through Creativity

BY SHIRLEY BARBOUR

A FRIEND HAS ASKED me if I am a scribe.

The dictionary defines a scribe as, "A person who made written copies of documents, before the invention of printing and in biblical times a teacher of religious law."

I asked that question to my team or guides. Here is what they said.

In particular, to the question on being a scribe, this is a state of writing that you are reading. You are receiving the information with allowance for what you are receiving. Different as you can see. This is a unique scribing for sure. Thus we should call this the exchange of a unique kind. Let us call this Divine Inspirational Writing.

I have been getting something about creation for three days. What can I say here about creativity and or creation?

Let us begin with the end in mind. There are many obstacles to creation if you listen to the general population. Creation can only be delved into or created from a logical set of principles inherent to the human population. Whereas Creation is a multi-dimensional thing and there needs to be a guiding principle in this.

Here in this time and in this place there are many who want to contribute to this writing. You can facilitate the expansion and the awareness of what this can be for humankind. There is an unveiling of how creation came about and there is much to tell you, learn, absorb and translate to you. Listen to our words as we transmit them to you, as there are many parts to the creation.

Let us start at the beginning and listen to your guidance!

What does that mean?

As a general guiding principle, this is where you listen. Most people never listen, so they never hear. It is joyful for us when you listen, so listen, we say.

How can I explain the concept of creation and creativity so it will assist the readers in getting or understanding what creation and creativity can contribute to our lives?

There is much to say here that will contribute to this understanding or the receiving of the information. In this ever-expanding universe there are those that contribute to creation and those that do not. We ask where you stand on creation and the creation process and we ask if you are here to create or are here to help others to create?

Being present with the energy of creation contributes to the actualization of it. What we mean by this is where our thoughts go, so does the energy. Create with caution so you are creating what will be an expansion of your world.

Being in the space of happiness and joy will create a space of joyful anticipation and allow for the creation to expand into. This allows what you are looking to create the ability to create.

When you are ready to create or to allow the creation to come into existence, you then have to allow for the generation of the thought to be transmuted into the universe where the energy is created for the thought to come into existence. Remember to always be ready to reach further than what you thought was possible. We call this the dynamics of the creation process, and thus where can you expand your dynamic and expansive ability to be in the creation process where we can contribute to what you are creating.

What does transmuted into the universe mean?

It is where you allow for the thought to change into the energetic vibration to create what you are asking for.

Can you simplify it for my readers?

We are here to help create a future for humanity and the collective to expand consciousness with ease. There can be no illusions about why we are here for the evolution for humanity. Therefore, this is a way for the general population to realize they can create and they can expand their life using the creation process. We will do our best to simplify how this is possible.

Remember that your thoughts create with the energy that they carry. Be the energetic vibration that you want to create.

Can you expand more on that?

When you create or think a thought you want to create, it carries a frequency of the thought. So when this frequency of the thought goes out into the universe to be created, it has to be a clear energy to create what you are asking for. With this clarity of thought there will be another positive change in the vibration, so you have to be very clear and precise in the asking. Be in the vibration of what you are asking for and allow for the thought to come into creation. Stay out of doubt or negative thoughts as this can hinder the process and also can negate what you are asking for altogether.

Is there a specific way to ask for what we want, when we are trying to create something?

Be specific and clear in your ask. Take out all fluffy words (filler words not specific to what you are asking for). When you create an "ask" as we call it, please remember that you are and have been creating all your life. Be not in doubt of what you are asking for as that negates the "ask".

Sometimes we think we want something, and then we change our mind when it does not appear right away. In the energy of creating what we are asking for, the universe has to rearrange things to create what you have been asking for. This can be instantaneous or can take some time. Be willing to wait and remember to ask again, not in the energy of doubt, stay in the energy of faith.

There are many ways to ask for what we want. Again, be specific, precise, use descriptive words.

Are there specific words that we can use in our "ask" to create what we want?

Fear not, use words that create for you what you require or desire in your life. There are many here to help with that. Let us begin.

I ask for abundance in (whatever you are asking for). It could be about finances, health, and your love relationship, anything you desire.

I ask for what would benefit me with the generation of allowance with this situation with my (son, daughter, friend, boss and or neighbor).

I ask for.... and so on!

I call what I do Connecting to Spirit. How can I share about how I connect?

We call it divine connection with the ever expanding consciousness of the universe. Where everything is available to access.

Where in this time and space can we all connect with ease to the cosmos and the universe at hand, with joyous anticipation? That is how everyone can connect. Just try, it can be a contribution.

There is a way to connect that will mostly be about divine inspiration that we talk about. Divine inspiration happens when we open our hearts to the possibility that we can connect, we can get answers. It starts with faith, the faith that we can and will receive an answer. This is where we will talk about opening the space for the answers to fall into.

What are the distinct ways to create?

There can be many avenues to create something. We say create what you love, create happiness, create play, create allowance, create joy, and from this space creation is easy. When we get into a space of joy, play, happiness and allowance, we create a space for creation to drop into. Therefore, let us create the space first.

How do you create the space?

Well, what makes you happy and joyful, and what can you do to be in allowance? There are many avenues you can take to get to the space. I get that some of you do not understand how to get there, or even want to get there. However, it is easy if you are willing.

Are you ready to create? We hear you say yes!

We say be careful what you wish for as creation can be instantaneous, or it can take a long time if you feel confused about what you want! Confused in your thoughts, they carry a frequency. This frequency of your thoughts creates your future. So what you think today creates your tomorrow.

Where in this time and space can we contribute to helping others bring into existence the things they would like to create!

What things can you assist or help create using the creation process?

You have to be able to do the work necessary to the development of the idea or thought on the topic you wish to create. This can include questions around art, painting, drawing, a document, a story, designing a website, just to name a few. Connecting to spirit can and will assist you with this endeavor.

Developing Your Inner Guidance System

Let us create a template or guidance system to help create an awareness of what wants to come in and to be ready, listen for the words.

There are many ways to create this, therefore you have to choose. So with this in mind, this is how we will start.

1. Be the space, be in allowance, be the awareness, be the laughter, the play, the acceptance and the joy of just being.

The space then opens somewhat like a door where you may feel, some may see, some hear, some may have an awareness of what they require.

2. Begin writing everything and anything you feel, you hear or are aware of. Be ready, allow and write or record, or type on a computer.

Some call this automatic writing, some call it using a Journal, and we call this divine inspiration, a joyful exuberance of love.

Sometimes when I am writing it is hard to differentiate between what I am thinking and what I am hearing or think I am hearing.

Write it down all the same, even your questions. Be in allowance of getting nothing and just leave the space and sit with it, as the space should be empty for the words, awareness and thoughts to fall into.

Sometimes I get one word at a time.

Just write it down and be in allowance of that.

The option I use when I am writing is speaking out loud as I record what I am saying, then I type it on the computer. However, it is more efficient to type as you record. Although some people like to write on paper, what option works for you?

We do not care how you do it, just that you do it. Be the expansion, be the space, and be the allowance!

3. Listen as you wait, do not fill the space, be willing to be in allowance, allow the silence, sitting in joyful anticipation.

This is a process, creation does not just happen, creation is created by our thoughts, and our willingness. Our willingness to receive! What are you willing to receive here that you have never been willing to receive before?

This can be a hard process if you are in avoidance and resistance with the receiving. There can be many times you will begin and then not listen and be in resistance, so thus no receiving happens. So resist not we say. If you are in the fear mode, just ask for help and it will be there instantaneously to support what you need or require. So be in the mode of trust with a dash of acceptance that this too will pass.

4. The frequency of love and joy and laughter is a beautiful space for the words, the information to fall into, therefore be joyful.

Be in love, be in the space of love, we mean. Readying the space with love and joy and laughter, play and allowance, is readying the space to receive the information into. There has to be a space and a place for the words to land, for you to receive it, so you can hear it, write it, perceive it, and type it. However you wish to do it, is up to you.

Therefore, the space, the place has to be ready! Are you ready and is the space filled with joy, love, laughter & play? Or is it stagnant, maybe something will happen, maybe not?

5. Allowance is key here! Listen, be willing to receive or not to receive, that's called allowance.

There are many factors to this receiving. There is listening, there is allowing, there is accepting, there is participating, there is anticipating and then again allowing from the anticipation.

Remember to start with the end in mind. We ask you, where are you not willing to receive and where are you not willing to allow yourself to receive? That carries forward into other areas of your life. It seems to be a natural occurrence. So we say be open to receiving.

That could be money, joy, love, and that could be a job. A cup of coffee, a bouquet of roses, a beautiful plant for your garden or your flower pot, a smile, just about anything.

6. Listen to your heart. Create from that space.

Listen, receive, be willing to receive, to hear or feel, or perceive, whatever way is right for you. Just because one person hears words does not mean that all will receive the information the same. Some people get an awareness, and some people it is just a knowing. Therefore, do what works for you! The key is to write! Feel in to the space, be ready and allow!

There are many people that will poo-poo what you do, share only if it feels right for you to share what you are doing.

Not all will want to know, and not everyone will hear you. Created for you, do it for you! If it creates more in the world that is what the aim here is.

Remember, you are a child of God and you are here to be what you're choosing to be, that will contribute to creating more for you. That will create for you, your life, your living, your family, your business, more of what you're willing to receive, would like to receive, and will allow yourself to receive.

Be in the space of allowance, awareness, willingness and the space of receiving to create a space for the information to fall into, drop into, received by you, for your betterment and the betterment (benefit) of humanity!

Listening is key here! Therefore, just fall into allowance! Fall in to that soft space, soft cloud, fluffy space, where you are in total allowance, while being aware of what you are creating.

7. Always be aware of what the energy is and set your space. I always ask for the information to come directly straight through me. From the divine light of God!

There can be many interlopers (spiritual interference not of the light) that can interfere with the process if you are not aware. Thus be willing to perceive a difference of the energy and be in non-allowance of that. Clear it so to speak, boot it out, whatever it may be. Be not in allowance of it and remember to set your space.

There are many modalities that can assist with clearing your space and or your body.

8. What is it you want to create or write about? If you don't know what you want to create, ask questions.

You sort this out first, unless you already have an awareness and something has been pinging you a few times. When you keep getting the same awareness, which is a sure-fire way of knowing that something wants to come through to be created. Just like with this chapter, I kept hearing the word creation for two or three days. While I was not sure what that was about: creation- the beginning of time, creation- creating something, creation- creating a book, creation- a book on creation, or a book creating a specific thing.

However, creation brought me to this chapter on developing your inner guidance system. That's all about creation. So do not make it finite, that it is a specific thing. Ask questions, and if you have the space and the allowance there, the answers will fall into that. It may not be today, it could be tomorrow or next week or one minute from now.

So you have to ask the questions, leave the space with the allowance, and the awareness that the answers will be coming.

Sometimes you can walk into a building and hear a piece of music and it is speaking to you. After my father died, at the funeral we listened to the music, a song by Louis Armstrong "What a Wonderful World". And for a few months after, there were days that I would go into a store and what was playing was "What a Wonderful World" and I would go somewhere else and low and behold it was playing again. Well, the song was letting me know that my Dad was around and I was not paying any attention. Just as some people say they kept finding pennies, so that would be normal for my Dad because he was a coin collector. It is being in the allowance and the awareness of those kinds of things to show up in your life for you to be, know, perceive and receive.

I hope that will facilitate you with the knowing that all is well as you create.

Listen, receive, allow, be receptive and all is well.

9. Keep asking questions if you are not getting an awareness or writing as that facilitates the process.

10. Using a journal sometimes helps as well to get your thoughts on paper. It can turn into automatic writing.

To sum things up or condense everything into a concise list below:

10 Ways Automatic Writing or Divine Inspiration can Open You up to Writing and Creating with Spirit.

Here are things you need to consider.

1. Be the space, be in allowance, be the awareness.

2. Write everything you feel, hear or are aware of.

3. Listen as you wait and do not fill the space, allow the silence.

4. Be the frequency of love and joy and laughter.

5. Allowance is key here. Be willing to receive or not to receive.

6. Listen to your heart. Create from that space.

7. Always be aware of what the energy is. Set your space.

8. Ask questions.

9. Ask more questions to generate more awareness, if not getting anything.

10. Use a journal daily for your thoughts. It can become automatic writing.

I started on the path of creating and writing with Spirit in about 2008, when I picked up and was reading a book by Doreen Virtue on "Angel Therapy". Then in early 2014 I connected with my son who had passed away in 1989. I will publish the story I am writing with my son in late fall. That story happened because I started doing a writing prompt and the story emerged from there. I did not believe my son was telling me the story until he helped me realize it through the writing process. So significant things can come from sitting and writing with Spirit.

Where in this time and space can we all connect with grace and understanding of the creation process and the ease it brings to what we are creating!

It is such a joy to connect with Spirit!

JOANN STEWART

JOANN STEWART HAS STUDIED various systems and traditions of astrology. However, once activated in 2012, and she began her awakening process, her perspective started changing as a result of her dramatic shift in consciousness.

Her approach combines traditional western astrology with ascension and quantum mechanics, polarity integration, architectural shifts, manifestation, the karmic field, Saturn-Moon matrix, and zero point mastery.

She writes a monthly astrological update, offers individual chart readings, and personal sessions focused on awakening, Ascension, and empowerment.

Joann also teaches small personalized groups her approach and understanding of astrology, the matrix, karmic field, timelines, separation of worlds (ascending vs. descending spiral), manifestation, divine union, unity consciousness, and zero point mastery.

How to find out more about Joann Stewart:

Her website is www.thesacredpath.co
You can reach out to her by email at info @thesacredpath.com

Breaking the Karmic Loop

BY JOANN STEWART

Since our planetary alignment with the galactic center and the opening of the ascension window in 2012, we have been in the transformational process of awakening, illumination and expansion of consciousness. Although deeply challenging, it's the only path of freedom, graduation through mastery, and exiting the matrix.

Awakening is more than just remembering, it's also the reclamation of power.

Ascension is part of our natural evolutionary process and involves (becoming whole again at the unified field).

We must break through many layers of amnesia and programming, while facing strong resistance and backlash from controlling entities that are part of the Negative Alien Agenda. We also have to make our way through the astral barriers and the 4th dimensional. This requires strong discernment, a steep learning curve, and dark arts training.

Emotionally this also requires healing and releasing our attachments to both fear and pain. Karmic relationships are based on fear, heavy programming; and the reluctance, and direct opposition, of (stepping out of the holographic black box). However, ascension offers the opportunity of choice: freedom over enslavement, and love over pain. We can align with the (ascending spiral), which is also our exit point out of (the matrix.)

Ascension is a natural process available during a window of time.

The Age of Pisces represents a culmination point, at the end of karmic cycles and the zodiac wheel. The separation of worlds provides a choice to evolve beyond 3rd dimensional consciousness, and the soul recycling program.

Awakening is destructive because it activates a monumental demolition project. The collective shift involves architectural changes that have a multidimensional ripple effect through time and space.

We are climbing out of a Dark Age and breaking through decrepit and parasitic structures. Controller forces have manipulated the collective consciousness through mind control, corrupting our human hologram corrupted and high jacking parts of the Cosmos through the Saturn-Moon matrix.

The karmic field is at the core of personalized programming used to trap humanity in a web of deception, exhaustion, and suffering. Only when we detach from the karmic web, and matrix feed-lines do we gain momentum on the road to freedom.

We are moving towards a bright new horizon, and a golden age for humanity, providing we leave the past behind. All of this requires spiritual maturity and taking personal responsibility as creators and cosmic citizens.

The return of Cosmic Christ Consciousness on the highly anticipated date of 12/21/12 initiated collective humanity into an accelerated process of awakening and revelation of truth. It is a truth revealed by light, only possible at the completion of cycles; and provides access to the galactic the galactic superhighway—the return of our future, our divine origins, and true selves. As with all graduations, there is intensive testing, and reflecting on what we have learned. It's also reunion time. We are reuniting within ourselves, and our divine counterparts. But we must detach from the karmic field which feeds into the black magic grid. The assortment of controller gatekeepers and repressive frequency nets will never willingly let us go. Only we can free ourselves when we remember our power and activate of our higher hearts and the divine spark of God-Source within.

Our awakening and ascension is cosmically orchestrated as we remember our divine origins. We have come to Earth to liberate a humanity that has been under the spell and death grip, of an anti-life agenda and vampiric consciousness. Through integrating higher frequencies and the light spectrum, we see again.

Astrology supports our process through a series of accelerated transits. The outer planets, specifically Pluto and Uranus, started activating the cardinal cross in June 2012, just prior to the opening of the ascension window. The cardinal signs are Aries, Cancer, Libra, and Capricorn. These are the initiators of the zodiac. We all have these signs in our charts. They represent areas of our lives, and the specifics of our ascension process; dismantled, transformed, and liberated from the matrix during the last 8 years. Our birth charts reflect our soul contracts and agreements. Pluto and Uranus play key roles in our ascension and activation of the cardinal cross. They impact areas of our charts that show rapid evolutionary change, illumination, and complete transformation.

Although very different, Pluto and Uranus work together effectively. They have been instrumental in our personal and collective process. Pluto, ruler of Scorpio, is the planet of death, rebirth, and transformation. It has been playing a powerful role in our emotional healing, and Dark Night of the Soul. Pluto forces us to face our shadows, heal, and look at what has been lurking deep in our subconscious mind. Uranus, ruler of Aquarius, represents cosmic consciousness, and activates the collective brain essentially through a process similar to electroshock therapy. It is the great awakener, shaking us from our slumber, and facilitating consciousness expansion. Pluto helps us transform through emotional purging, healing, and releasing all that stands in our way of freedom. Uranus sends us a lifeline and lightening rod of higher frequency and light spectrum.

While this is an intense and overwhelming process; in the earlier phases it is necessary to remove veils of illusion and snap out of the collective spell. We become lucid dreamers, and remember it is our dream, and our collective hologram. We also see through the smoke and mirrors of the black magic grid.

Understanding karma and the karmic field during our awakening is important. The karmic field feeds into the black magic grid, which traps humanity in a vampiric web of deception and satanic ritual. The global cult feeds into a parasitic consciousness, siphoning energy through artificial feed lines and satanic grid. The human collective animates the system, providing life force to an otherwise dead zone. It bases the holographic world stage of 3D reality on bi-wave architecture and a death culture. Unless we detach from the karmic grid and seal previous vulnerabilities, we still feed the system. The artificial overlay and assortment of karmic gatekeepers, hold humanity hostage, trapped on the descending spiral. Over time, during our interaction with the karmic field, we develop unnatural addictions and attachments to drama, suffering, and pain-pleasure reversals. We stay lost in the lower 3 chakras, below the astral barrier. We associate love with pain and suffering in relationships as the norm.

The Dark Night of the Soul is a spiritual initiation, and although deeply painful, is a very productive phase of awakening. It facilitates a tremendous amount of healing and revelation of truth; about ourselves, our history, and the multidimensional nature of reality. This Dark Night dismantles old identities, beliefs, and programming attachments. In its earlier phases, all that we have identified with as ourselves and our reality, collapses around us. However, it's only the illusionary and artificial aspects and creations that collapse: not our attachments to them. This is positive and required if we are to transcend 3rd dimensional consciousness and break through the astral barrier. The deconstruction of an old world, while rebuilding a new one, is a messy, and sometimes surreal process. The result is freedom, empowerment and liberation of one's self and the human species.

Prior to our awakening, our perception of reality and the manifested world was based on societal programming, karmic entrapment, and enslavement to an externalized authority. The matrix feed-lines plugged into the collective consciousness and were redirected into holding tanks and vampiric consciousness. This was the ultimate, nefarious, pyramid scheme that worked against humanity, benefiting members of a global satanic cult. As we collectively awaken, the truth is revealed and corrected by a higher authority based on cosmic sovereign law. Cosmic justice is on our side and the controllers have no creative capacity of their own. They maintain the illusion of power through the harvesting of energy, and high jacking of human consciousness.

Our collective hologram is what we perceive as reality on the physical plane. It's the last step in the process of manifestation, like a domino effect which begins in the higher time fields and works its way down. Corrupted over time, our collective hologram engulfed the consciousness of a sleeping population. The negative alien agenda and parasitic consciousness that fed off humanity is losing their food source, and their power, as more people awaken. When we collectively break through our fears and realize our true power, there is no stopping this process. During our slumber we forgot that it's our dream, and collective hologram. We started taking orders from external authorities and looking outside ourselves for the knowledge that is actually within. We forgot that our external landscape, and 3D playing field, reflects our inner world. To manifest from a place of clarity and authentic mastery, we have to remove all the clutter of matrix programming, filters, implants, and wounding that diverts our focus and natural creative abilities.

The original hologram differed from it is now. It was more cohesive, harmonious—a seamless flow of conscious co-creation. We are in a collective dream and awaken as the lucid dreamer.

Awakening and ascension are demanding processes with ongoing and accumulative phases of dismantling, healing, rebirth and expansion. They require incredible strength, tenacity, and endurance. To make it through requires transcendence and mastery and the courage to leave the past behind.

The karmic field provides an assortment of roles, archetypes, and direct oppositions. After the planetary invasion and installation of artificial technology, the karmic field was weaponized and used to trap humanity. The negative alien agenda—the ultimate computer virus in the collective consciousness—controlled our thoughts and beliefs and entrained the human collective through the installation of energetic computer software programming.

Everything about our reality, and the human experience, inverted over time along with the corruption of our hologram. The karmic web of deception, and consciousness entrapment, is at the core of human suffering. Prior to the ascension window, we had no access to memories. Our attempts to achieve harmony, or connection, in karmic inter-personal dynamics has been repeatedly met with conflict, gaslighting, and direct opposition. The karmic net is a false love software program keeping us in consciousness lockdown. It interconnects with the false god religious programming, which is also abusive, and temperamental, inciting fear, and demands subservience.

Our process of awakening provides the strength and self-love to transcend the astral barrier in the 4th dimension, and the holographic control structures and negative entities. Our attachments to the karmic field are a roadblock to ascension. It's clever set trap, kept powerful creator beings, born with the divine spark of pure life force, trapped in a cage. The karmic field feeds into the black magic grid, and energy holding tanks, consumed by a negative alien agenda, and parasitic consciousness that revolves around AI reversal systems. Humanity's fear of death is a mind control program within in a death culture. It's like being afraid of going to prison while already incarcerated.

Our future beyond the Matrix is open and free. It is available now in the higher time fields. We have to see beyond the illusions and unravel from our own self-deceptions. When we understand that genuine love is real and accessible now during our reunion process, we evolve beyond the Matrix. There is nothing normal, or even human about karmic relationships. They are computer programs based on drama, suffering, manipulation, and fear. The difficulties of karmic situations, and pain-pleasure reversals, keeps us recycling in unresolvable emotional patterns, and energetic whiplash. Because of the holographic design of karmic relationships, they perpetuate a sense of loneliness and self-defeat. They serve the Matrix system via feed-back loop and have nothing to do with love. During the bifurcation and separation of worlds, we are moving from bi-wave architecture to trinity wave.

Trinity wave, and divine union, is the return to zero point mastery, and unconditional love within ourselves and our divine counterpart. We are leaving karmic relationships behind and exhausting cycles of opposition and polarity.

The process of ascension is a beautiful process of mastery, empowerment, wholeness, and genuine unconditional love at the unified field of zero point.

EARTH SONG

EARTHSONG IS AN INTUITIVE Energy Alchemist & Ceremonialist who utilizes Reiki, Sound Healing, Earth Medicines & Ceremony to help her clients transform their relationship with themselves, understand their energetic nature, and live in alignment with their soul's purpose. She specializes in helping her clients cultivate and embrace unconditional self-love, respect, and recognition of worth.

Utilizing the transformational power of Ceremony is one of Earth-Song's favorite ways to help people connect deeply with themselves, the Earth and the Divine. Her current Ceremonial passion is sharing the plant medicine of Theobroma Cacao. Years of communion with this plant medicine has led EarthSong on a journey of profound heart healing. Cacao resonates with the heart chakra and offers healing for the body, mind, and spirit – it brings healing in a way that is gentle and subtle, yet powerful and expansive.

EarthSong has navigated the complexities of her shadows and understands the intricacies of healing our physical and energetic traumas. Her journey through healing has taught her the value of discernment and the skill of listening to one's self to discover our truths.

"There is no rushing the healing process and the best lessons are learned when we *honor the ebb and embrace the flow*".

How to find out more about Earth Song:
www.SoulfullyAuthentic.com
Instagram: @SoulfullyAuthentic
FB: https://www.facebook.com/SoulfullyAuthentic

Ceremony as Therapy:
Energy Alchemy to Transform Your Life

BY EARTH SONG

I sat there on the floor in a circle of women, looking down at the words I wrote. Tears flowing down my cheeks and falling off my chin.... as a deluge of emotions released the pressure of over two decades of dis-ease, collecting in a pond on the floor at my feet.

I hear a voice in my head: "Who am I?"

Three simple words that, when arranged in this order, were not simple at all. Three simple words that provided clarity and a sense of impending doom. Although the realization that I did not understand who I was, hit me like a ton of bricks, it also gave me some insight into the general malaise that had overtaken me in the last 6 months.

"Who am I?" The question stuck with me. I could answer who I was for everyone else; wife, mother, friend, daughter... but who I was for myself, I had no answer. This moment and this question were turning points in my life. I knew I was at the beginning of a quest for self-discovery that would bring healing and clarity, but I did not know how it would all play out. I had no clue that Ceremony would be a major player in my story! And that Ceremony would be my greatest therapy!

An Awakening

The "Who am I" question came to me while attending a retreat for new mothers. I was 11 months postpartum and lost! Like so many new (and not so new) moms, I was trying to figure out how I fit into this world. And, although I came to this question after giving birth, I knew the weight it carried was exacerbated by the realization that I had been subconsciously asking myself this question my entire life.

The retreat was my first introduction to sitting in a circle with women and to Sacred Ceremony (not the watered-down mainstream gatherings I had experienced to date). Though challenging, it was a breath of fresh air and the first step of my Healer's Journey.

That weekend I opened my eyes to a world of rituals, ceremony and magic that I had yet to experience in my actual life. Cleansing the body with sacred smoke, calling upon the seven directions for guidance and protection, and meditating to meet guides and ancestors alchemized my pain into medicine. I aligned my body and soul with a world and way of being that I had not known was possible. My spirit awakened from a hibernation so deep; I had not even known it existed.

I attended many of these retreats over the next 18 months, each time digging deeper, exposing wounds; knowing and healing myself more. Each time the retreat ended with a deep sadness that the "magic was over". I wanted to LIVE this magic... Connected to my SELF and the wisdom of our great Mother Earth. I craved a sacred way of being.

Defining Sacred Ceremony

Take a moment to pause and reflect on the following questions:

When you hear the word Ceremony, what images come to mind for you?

In your life, what Ceremonies have you experienced and how have you connected with them? Physically? And emotionally?

I had a limited view of Ceremony, prior to my profound journey within it. Growing up in a suburban, white, middle class family, I thought Ceremonies were formal events such as weddings, christenings, or funerals. Or they were some mystical, inaccessible ritual from a land and culture I was not a part of...

What if Ceremony was more than what mainstream western society presents it as? What if Ceremony was something we looked forward to as an opportunity to connect with ourselves and others? Ceremony is a way of being in this world that is profoundly healing! Ceremony is therapeutic, assisting those who are open and willing to transform the way they think, feel, and interact with themselves and the world at large.

When I refer to Sacred Ceremony in this writing, I am describing Ceremony that we may hold and or attend intending to connect with something greater than our physical selves. Whether you feel most comfortable with the label Higher Self, Infinite Spirit, God, the Universe, Mother Earth or the Divine, does not matter. What is most important is that the term you use resonates with your current understanding of reality. I will use many of these terms in this writing as I have cultivated appreciation and awareness with them throughout my spiritual evolution and Ceremonial practices.

Each Ceremony has its own unique intention, purpose, and goals. Connection to the Divine is the common thread that makes Sacred Ceremony Sacred. Without recognition of the Divine, ceremony is just a celebration, or sometimes, a ritual. I believe that Ceremony, ritual, and celebration are all vital aspects of our human existence, each holding a special place in my heart.

Learning Sacred Ceremony

In 2015, I embarked on a quest to learn, embody, and live as the Healer I discovered hidden away deep inside myself. It led me to

Earth Medicine School. The three years of study that followed were soul awakening, transformative & empowering!

I then connected with my Self, the natural world and Spirit, moving beyond my physical reality to realms far beyond anything I could have imagined or comprehended. It was during self-exploration with Earth Medicine teachings that I was first introduced to the practice of Sacred Ceremony. Sacred Ceremony was a balm for my tired, forgotten soul! It was the nourishment I did not know I needed.

I believe that the dis-ease that we suffer stems from our detached state of being. Our mainstream, modern world gives little value to establishing, nurturing, and maintaining authentic, meaningful connections. Ceremony gives us a container to discover and foster connection: connection to our physical and spiritual selves, our community, to the Earth, our Ancestors and the Divine.

The therapy of Ceremony exists not only in the connections we discover and strengthen but also the experience of equality within a circle, the practice of vulnerability with ourselves and others, and the permission to alchemize our pain into medicine.

Healing Our Lost Connections

Ceremony is ALL about connections. One connects with the Higher Self, fellow humans, the Earth, ancestors, Spirit and the Universe with each Ceremonial encounter. Losing our sacred connections leads to a suffering that is so commonplace that we consider it an ordinary state of being. Dismembered by time and materialism, we forget how to foster and grow our divine connections. We suffer believing we are alone, so disconnected from our Self, that we cannot hear the whispers of our soul.

Many of us grew up in households and cultures that invalidated our divinity and the sacredness of the Earth. Ceremony gives us a container for going beyond the physical and into the mystic—the magical realms where the medicine of authentic connection lives. Healing our lost connections to ourselves, our community, the Infinite Spirit and the Earth are the foundation of becoming who we are here to be and aligning with our wholeness and purpose.

Each time I attend a Ceremony or sit in a sacred circle, I become more whole. Sometimes that means I recover a lost part of myself. But more often it is more subtle, the wholeness or re-remembering comes in the form of clarity... gaining insight on who I am, who I want to be and how I want to show up in this world. It is less like finding a missing piece of my puzzle... It is more like a distorted, forgotten piece of my essence, heals. It comes into focus and transforms its shape, now able to fit into my current state of being. My energetic system updates affecting my whole being.

When we experience trauma, a piece of our energy or soul often sticks to the time and space of the event. Dissociation happens as a protective mechanism when we are incapable of processing an event at the time of its occurrence. Problems arise when we cannot recover ourselves fully, which leads to reliving experiences and repeated unproductive patterns. Full healing from a traumatic event occurs when we recover parts of our self that we left behind.

Our Ancestors

Ceremony stokes the flames of our antiquity. For our ancestors, Ceremony and ritual were a vital part of the human experience. The purpose and function of Ceremony may have differed across cultures and throughout time, but Ceremony was a common occurrence in our ancestor's lives.

When we take part in Ceremony, we commune with our ancestors. We tap into a way of being that is familiar and understood by them regardless of our heritage. Our ancestors sit with us, offer guidance, support, and unconditional love.

When we take part in Ceremony, we not only heal ourselves but also our ancestors and our future descendants: energy is not linear and not bound by space and time in the same ways our human bodies are.

My Ceremonial work with the plant medicine Theobroma Cacao—a master heart healer, assists me in cultivating a practice of unconditional love of self and others. Through this practice I help release my ancestors from their chains of conditional love and lack of worth, while also fostering a practice of infinite love and recognition of their value for generations yet to come.

Equality

A Circle has no beginning and no end. One of the significant powers of Ceremony is the egalitarianism of sitting in a circle. Although someone leads the ceremony, they sit in the circle as an equal. They are "in the experience" with you and everyone in attendance. The practice and reality of equality within a group can seem foreign and uncomfortable for some. In ceremony, you must do your own inner work. The facilitator is a guide but is not there to heal you—you are the director of your healing. Healing comes easily with the willingness to be vulnerable, claim our power and our shadows, recognize our stories and trust that the experiences we have are for our greatest good.

Vulnerability

When was the last time you allowed your authentic self to be seen & heard—your true essence witnessed without judgement or the need to fix? Have you allowed this to happen by you, to you? Looked in the mirror and been witness instead of critic?

The evolution of a more solitary existence affects our ability to be vulnerable in community. We witness vulnerability on TV or in movies, but exposing ourselves in real-life relationships is limited. The absence of exposure to the energy of vulnerability when being physically present with it, compounds the discomfort we experience when even thinking about being vulnerable with ourselves or others.

Vulnerability is a learned skill. Expressing our vulnerability and witnessing that of others is discouraged in adolescence because our parents were not taught how to be open themselves. We are conditioned to strive for perfection (which does not exist) rather than authenticity. We become so disconnected from ourselves that we can not even tap into and name our authentic emotions and feelings.

Regardless of all the "therapies" available today, at its core, therapy is most successful when we access our vulnerability... Ceremony as therapy is no different. Trust in the facilitator and the process is a requirement. You must walk the journey not knowing where you are being led or what your destination will be. As soon as the soul says YES to Ceremony, supportive energies such as your spiritual guides/team swing into action. This provides you with the experience you need—rarely is it the experience you expect.

As a facilitator of ceremony and sacred gatherings, I witness countless spiritual and emotional breakthroughs, breakdowns and transformations that bring deep profound healing and peace. These alchemical expeditions take place when participants embrace vulnerability and befriend their shadows.

Community

Sitting in Ceremony feeds and nourishes our spirit in a way few other things in this earthly existence can. When we sit in Ceremony, we sit in community. We sit with strangers, relatives, friends or partners. People we may have never come into contact with in this lifetime, in any other way, link to us and us to them, even if we never meet again.

With each ceremonial experience, we change. Witnessing peoples' pain and triumph, we share experiences, and realize how similar we all are. We learn from the stories and lessons of others and convey our own bringing forth that which is ready for healing within us. The energy of others—mingling our energy with theirs, creates a new energy, shared among us. We carry this with us long after we go our separate ways. This is one of the greatest gifts of Ceremony.

Ceremonial Alchemy

Each time we gather in a Sacred Ceremony we transform. The energetic alchemy that takes place during Ceremony creates shifts in our consciousness, our humanness, and our souls. These shifts change us in ways we do not understand or recognize. The continuum of transformation we ride with each energetic encounter creates a ripple effect, not only for us, but one that radiates into the ethers and reverberating all dimensions of time and space.

When we open ourselves to the therapy of Ceremony, we can be "here" and also see beyond the present. We see past the physical, feel into our traumas, open up to the energy of our souls, and see ourselves as the whole and unique creatures we are. We adopt gratitude for all the strands of our life experience, for these have birthed us as the magical creatures we are today.

To receive the alchemy of Ceremony, you must embrace vulnerability. Allowing ourselves to be witnessed authentically in a safe community is one of the best gifts we can ever give ourselves. When embrace and share the raw and real beautiful messes we are, we give others permission to do the same. We ALL benefit!

Ceremony has been a catalyst for significant change in my life. It has been my greatest therapy. The alchemy of my traumas and expansion of spirit that occurred were possible because I could trust and allow. My trust in the Universe's timing, my teachers, my vulnerability, and Higher Self allowed me to experience the alchemical qualities of Ceremony fully and completely.

As an Intuitive Healer, Energy Alchemist and Ceremonialist, I am on a sacred mission to bring Ceremony back into the mainstream; as a way of alchemizing our wounds so we can live in embodied wholeness and help our culture reclaim its therapeutic and medicinal qualities.

Will you join me?

CHRISTIE GRANT

CHRISTIE GRANT IS A registered nurse with over 26 years treating clients with mental health challenges. She is skilled in traditional talk therapies. Her primary specialty is supporting families of youth, with eating disorders towards recovery.

Christie has also spent the last 50 years exploring the invisible realms and the nature of reality as it impacts our day-to-day lives. From traditional religions to esoteric spirituality, she has trained in many energetic and intuitive modalities.

Christie's talent lies in weaving traditional mental health practices with leading edge energetic modalities. This allows her clients to create a firm foundation of wholeness that empowers authentic self-expression and a more open hearted, joyful approach to life. Through aligning with their body's intelligence and a more positive self-regard, deep transformation is possible.

Her passion and pleasure are offering transformative tools for clients to achieve a happier, abundant life through focused body positivity and self-love. As Christie moves into retirement from clinical treatment, she looks forward to working with clients in a more deeply spiritual practice connecting them to the God within and their soul's purpose.

How to find out more about Christie Grant:

Her website is http://christiegrant.com/

Your Emotions as a Pathway to the Divine

BY CHRISTIE GRANT

"Within us is a secret longing to remember the light, to step out of time in this dancing world. It's where we began and it's we return."
Jack Kornfield

THROUGHOUT TIME WE HAVE yearned for something "more" than our mundane lives, an intrinsic knowing that there must be more to life than meets the eye. Something to give all the suffering a greater meaning. From the beginning we have looked up to the stars and delved deeply within ourselves for answers to these questions. This chapter will explore working with your emotions as an avenue to achieving greater peace and clarity with these inner longings.

"Emotions??" you say? "Why would I want to do that?!!" Emotions are messy, often disturbing and distressing! How can that lead to enlightenment?" The answer is simple yet often overlooked in our culture that values thought and logic over feeling.

Eckhart Tolle, the modern mystic, coined the term "the pain body" to describe that part of us that hides deep psychological pain. Pain is an inevitable part of life that occurs when something

117

disturbing or traumatic happens to us. We don't like to feel it and our psyche instinctively pulls back - like when we physically pull our hand back from something hot. We experience this as an increase in bodily tension or psychological constriction in the heart. We become scared of feeling the pain, so we become invested in avoiding it and create whole narratives about what happened and why we need to behave in certain ways.

This avoidance is so commonplace in our culture; we don't even question it, despite the huge cost to our happiness and freedom. It's well known in mental health circles that most mental health disorders are based on patterns of emotional avoidance. In my twenty-five years as a psychiatric nurse, most of the mental health clients and patients I worked with hold on to deeply buried, unfelt emotional pain. To avoid feeling this pain, they arranged their lives; creating all kinds of neurosis and maladaptive coping strategies such as addiction, eating disorders, anxiety and mood disorders. They didn't realize that trying to avoid feeling their painful emotions kept them unchanged within themselves.

The important thing to know is that emotions are temporary sensations that have a lifespan. They occur as reactions that tell us how something has affected us; whether it's an external event or a thought. If allowed to move through the body unencumbered, emotions run their course and cease to be. Period! Just knowing that their intensity will end, can allow us to be more courageous in facing them. However, when we don't allow this natural flow through the body, emotions stay in our energetic field and nervous system as ramped up energy that creates tension waiting for release. They stay, they do not leave or change into something more peaceful. And though held emotion becomes buried under layers of rationalization, we continue to experience that pain as negative emotions, reactivity and judgements in too many of our day-to-day interactions.

Most spiritual development involves making peace with this pain. How do we do that? Michael singer in his groundbreaking work *The Untethered Soul*, describes an effective process for doing this.

First, decide that you don't want the fear of pain to run your life anymore. Sit with your pain quietly and feel first the sensation of tension in your body, especially in your heart area: then relax and breathe, despite any resistance that arises. You will feel strong sensations arising in your body and perhaps traumatic memories that link to the pain. If the latter occurs, working with a skilled therapist is a good idea to provide a safe, supported space and additional skills to resolve them.

A client of mine had a similar experience. She had experienced significant sexual abuse as a young teen and had borne scars from this for several years. When we did the relax and breathe exercise, she experienced strong sensations in her body and visual and auditory memories of the abuse. By creating a safe space in the shared experience and guiding her with breathing, she felt the increased and decreased intensity of the body sensations and relief from the bodily felt pain at the end. Then came an upwelling of sadness and grief at the loss of the hoped for happy adolescence and anger at her parents for not protecting her. As we worked through those feelings in additional sessions, she could say the abuse had less and less power over her and she was no longer terrified of the memories.

Eckhart Tolle, in *The Power of Now,* suggests trying to separate any story you have associated with your painful emotions. Put the story aside as best you can and just feel the physical sensations in your body. You will notice the sensations increasing in intensity. This will create unpleasant discomfort that can feel overwhelming or just intense. When I observe my clients carefully, I've noticed a tendency to shut down or come out of the breathing because they feel fear. But if I can guide them to stay present and relaxed by focusing on their breathing, something remarkable happens. They tell me that the sensations continue to build and eventually peak, then gradually dissipate. I notice their body relaxes more deeply. They report the emotion changed to something more positive or disappeared altogether.

It's important to stay with the exercise until you feel some release, whether it be deep relaxation, heaving sighs, or crying. Then the payoff comes; a deeper feeling of calm and clarity about what that emotion has been trying to tell you. Sometimes it might just be an awareness of how strongly an event or thought has affected you. Or it might yield increased clarity about how the negative judgements are creating obstacles to feeling happier and more peaceful. Clients often tell me they feel drained and tired afterwards and need to rest to integrate the changes.

You may need to do the focused breathing exercise for brief periods initially to build your tolerance for feeling the distress that comes with feeling painful emotions. And that's OK - there's no right or wrong here. If you find it's too overwhelming or feels too unsafe, you might need to engage with a therapist or energetic healer to assist you.

Emotions are always an accurate reflection of how something has affected us whereas our thoughts are not. When you realize that you won't die and that your life won't implode if you feel distressing emotions, they cease to have the same power over you. You feel stronger and more sure of yourself. Then it's easier to approach and fully feel them when they occur instead of avoiding them. There's no build-up of psychic pressure that leads to anxiety and depression. Understanding their message can provide clarity about what to do next. And that gives you more power to make decisions instead of reacting blindly to unconscious emotional triggers.

Emotional healing transforms the energy body by opening the heart. If we also support our bodies with loving kindness and healthy life-style choices, they can hold higher vibrational frequencies required to embody advanced states of consciousness. For example, the higher yogic pursuits of kundalini and tantra can raise the frequencies in our bodies through movement and breath. These act as a doorway to higher states of bliss and conscious awareness. Using alcohol and other drugs or ingesting food with low nutritional value impedes this process.

Spiritual practices such as studying inspirational texts, meditation, and introspection can focus our attention and intention to allow our highest good however we imagine it.

When we delve into ourselves through meditation, we discover a deeper aspect of ourselves that is eternal. This is our true "Self" the consciousness aware of our thoughts that feels our emotions and receives input from our senses. When we reach that deep quiet place within ourselves we realize we are not our experiences but the observer of them.

Bodies are physical entities run by biochemical and bio-electric processes that are both physical and energetic. Everything has consciousness and energy: our bodies do, our thoughts do, and our emotions do. It took me a long time to accept that my body has its own consciousness and system of needs which differ from my mental mindset of opinions and beliefs.

Our thoughts, feelings, emotions and bodies are our own creation. However, these are affected by the collective thoughts, emotions and energies of humanity. Even though we are born with the genetics and other characteristics of our parents, we are distinct from them in terms of personality and behavioral choices. Just compare yourself to your siblings to see how true this is.

Pain is an indicator that something is not right and needs our attention. We avoid it because of beliefs that it will increase suffering or that it will last forever. Our avoidance of emotional pain is a major stumbling block to uniting with God. In *Mary Magdalene Beckons, Join the River of Light,* Mercedes Kirkel suggests, "Rather than seeing pain or a "no" as proof that we've been abandoned, we can see them as God's way of beckoning us and use them as a pathway to re-embrace God".

Pain is a sign that we have disconnected from God within ourselves. When we face our emotional pain without flinching or negative self judgement, and let it roll through us, we realize that we are not our pain, but so much more. We transcend our limiting beliefs and understand that we are all connected through both our shared human experience and our potential to transcend the illusion of separation and experience bliss.

Many of my clients report an expansion and a lightening in their being: they can perceive expanded aspects of themselves after receiving energetic clearings and healing touch. They understand that their painful experiences are just that—experiences that they are having rather than who they are. Once they have connected with their true self deep inside, the impact of their traumatic experiences dissipates.

The diversity of life masks the underlying unity of all existence. Just as the wave flowing over our feet is not separate from the ocean, we are all one in consciousness. When we have a transcendent experience of this, we experience it through our body with sensations that are both body-based and at a vibration that transcends the body and blurs its edges. This awareness brings peace and higher vibrational emotions of joy, courage and others.

Often, we feel alone, misunderstood and unsupported because of our unhealed wounding. Guidance and support are always available for us through prayer and our intuition. This comes from God and higher beings of light who are here to help us.

"You are not alone. You are never alone. This the greatest challenge for human beings to learn. It is the challenge of being born as a seemingly separate individual. We are with you always. Just call upon us and we are here. We are powerful and we for your highest good" (*Mary Magdalene Beckons, Join the River of Light*).

When you ask for help with an open heart, you can expect guidance in terms of what to do next to both heal yourself and solve other problems. It can come in many forms, such as a flash of insight, or the small voice in our minds, even the writing on the side of a truck. For example, recently I put my house up for sale and then the Covid-19 quarantine set in. No one came to view the house or felt comfortable putting in an offer. I wondered if I should take it off the market until the quarantine lifted. I prayed daily for guidance on what to do and kept getting a sense of confidence that it would sell and to persist with the listing. I kept clearing negative energies and downloading light and love into the house. Daily, I set a powerful intention to draw the right buyer at the right time with a good offer for the highest good of all involved. Within six weeks I received an acceptable offer and I am now in the process of moving out.

According to Mary Magdalen, we will know that it is true guidance "if it sustains your peace and keeps your heart open" (*Mary Magdalene Beckons, Join the River of Light*). That was the case for me. I felt uplifted and joyful in moving forward in my life.

This is the goal in working with our emotional pain. When we resolve it, we remove another obstacle to feeling always connected to God. This is what we have been looking for in our longing for something to give deeper meaning to our lives. We are not separate from God and we are all connected in God. Because of this, we can take heart in knowing that feeling our emotional pain can lead us to freedom from it, and that guidance is always available to us if we just ask. The path through emotional pain is difficult but is so worth it because it strengthens us and leads us to greater peace, self-love and self-acceptance.

CHASTITY KRIBBLE

CHASTITY IS A STARSEED guide and healer offering classes and personal sessions to assist during the ascension cycle. She helps to awaken dormant memories and codes within the multidimensional selves awakening the architect in each of us.

You can find out more about Chastity here:

Here website is https://www.theartofmetta.com
Chastity Kribble Youtube: https://bit.ly/3e2qSJz
https://www.instagram.com/theartofmetta/
https://www.patreon.com/frequencyhealing
https://m.facebook.com/theartofmetta/

VOICE OF THE GUIDES:
CLEARING THE SHADOW SELF AND THE EGO

BY CHASTITY KRIBBLE

MY CHAPTER STARTS WITH a story. A little girl, if you will standing in the shadows frightened of the things she has witnessed, will witness. She has a sense of knowing far beyond her time spent on this planet, in this life or lifetime, you might say. She can hear and see the unknown; life is full of colors, voices, and beings. Beings you can only imagine or have seen on the television.

We bring this up because one person's truth should not stand in the way of another's beliefs or progress through their particular life cycle, or a lifetime—the sequences of life.

When she comes here, she takes on a perspective from the world; the entire planet mapped upon her body. There are codes and mini maps to the secrets of the whole universe with every little detail the eyes, skin, body shape, into the neurons and blood.

This little girl is me.

I have never tried to channel a writing piece from my guides, but it is how I teach my classes. I will be communicating with my guides, and as they answer questions or speak through me, I will write. The text you read will be transformational for each person in different ways. Please find a comfortable space, relax, and let us begin our journey together.

CODES

When she asks of shadows, she says, why are people standing in them? Is it separate from the self?

The answer is no; the self creates it. By the constructs, that man has created and defined as self.

There's an eerie simplicity to attaining knowledge, a simplistic viewpoint.

You have the right to choose.

That is always what I say.

Yes, but what one continues to choose is harmful, most often binding themselves into the lower dimensions of enslavement. Do you see what we mean?

Yes, but how do we explain this to others. Simplicity does not go over well with people. We seem to believe everything has to be hard to be effective. Then if it's too hard, it's easy to give up.

The shadow construct can be healed when one can recognize the shadow as self and not separate from self. Many of you believe the darkness is to be avoided and cast it away. When you look at the darkness in the world, we must see that it is attached to self. To heal and help the planet, we support the self. By facing the darkness with our inner light, we heal.

As I write, I can see my demons rising to the surface. The guides have stepped back for me to see this in full view. These are ideas or constructs I have created to bind myself to the false reality that what I have to share or birth into the world will never do, that it isn't enough that it will never be enough, and the reason is that I didn't know enough.

Now here is the truth we want you to see; the houses of the ego you have built are many. They will crumble beneath your feet when you recognize them just as you did at this moment. You could feel the rumbling and warm sensations through your body, and vibrations change once you faced those demons, as you say, or construct of reality. It crumbled to the ground. Now you can build a new.

In all fairness to you, the reader, I have recognized ego, the shadow self, for many years. As layers slough away, new ego emerges. The longer we work with these frequencies, the easier it is to clear at the moment you sense it arise. Be kind to yourself as new truths push through to the surface of your consciousness. Love is the answer to all things. The light you each hold will transform even the ugliest and devastating realities to the surface.

Kindness was the most significant gift the guides had me unwrap. I learned first to be kind to myself. I extended myself the grace needed when I wasn't perfect, and through the dark times, love was the light I saw.

I want to tell each of you that the journey is simple, that it will happen quickly. That would not be true. For some of you, self-realization may promptly lead to self-actualization, and for others, it will be a painful struggle. It will be a battle of truth, lies, memories, and the realization that you will never be the same again.

Self Mastery 101

Forget everything you know to be the truth. I am serious. Remove the idea that you are the busy loving mom with no time for herself or the father that works too much to see his kids or the one who makes everybody smile. These are all things you have chosen to identify through. Belief systems create realities.

I remember when I was a young girl I spent hours trying to understand why a toilet was a toilet or a chair, a chair. What if I wanted it to be called something else? I didn't comprehend who and why somebody else got to choose what everything in my world was named. Eventually, I gave up asking questions as nobody had answers, and over time, my creativity was tucked away nicely in the ethers to hopefully never discover again.

Here are my guides stepping back in.

You believe the realities set upon you in any given moment.

What does that mean?

Each of you are a sounding board for truth, a vibration that echos in the ethers, one must call back their true form and rise like a phoenix from the ashes. The truth never lies. Darkness cannot hold the light; it is the light that transforms the darkness. These words mean something. You asked previously if the text (this chapter) can "mean" something to the reader. Transformation can happen through the vibration of the words that each chooses to accept. The codes, if you will carry vibration as you write from your heart center with the intention of self-actualization and the transformation to the reader. The ego construct will fall away when the truth appears that the ego exists. Self-knowing will be the first step. Knowing. Knowing that you have operated from a low vibration by design and without your knowledge.

How can we help the reader understand what this means?

The realization of self is one of the most complex constructs we have created. As mentioned earlier, this is a reality that can be re-known.

In the knowing, we must create the time needed to cultivate a new relationship with what we believed to be true about the self. With this knowledge, a new reality will actualize.

Calling in my higher self has become more comfortable as time passes. It's nearly effortless. With the mind clear, we can stand in zero point, the god matrix, making anything possible. I believed this as a child, then I had forgotten. Over the years, I asked to remember, and I have awakened to remember it again. The Zero

Point is the God Matrix field. Here is a short excerpt the ascension glossary;

Love is a radiating, strengthening and unifying force spiralling into the upward movement towards the central point of Oneness, the Zero Point. The Force of Love naturally aligns itself back into unity with the Zero Point Field, the unified heart of the Universe. The absence of love, or hatred, is a disintegrating, separative and weakening force, which absorbs light and energy away from the central point of Oneness. (*ascensionglossary.com*)

The Zero Point is where I anchor in my protection shield, which allows higher frequencies to aid in the ascension of my multidimensional self. Being protected and anchored is essential when shadow/negative ego begins to rise. We have entangled ourselves into a masterpiece of deception. The web of lies pulsating through the feet, and out the crown, has created the ego constructs we live through.

We are in a global crisis and have been for centuries. The most current crisis has shaken millions of us to awaken to the truth, to awaken the shadow. The program of deception and lies our consciousness is running on has been uncovered. For those who choose to see, life will never be the same again. We are going through a planetary Dark Night of the Soul, a purging of darkness and of "things" that no longer serve us. As ego clears, our lives shift to hold the new frequencies that are coming in. The changes can be devastating and frightful.

Is there anything to add to the reader?

Many cannot understand, and many still choose to turn a blind eye. For each of you, we hold space for compassion and for the light pillars of truth to be your beacon of hope. This transmission is of love and peace. Beloveds continue to break down the walls you have built your reality through. The constructs of peace lie within your hearts. The memories are in your dreams as you soar high above the winds, and as you come back down, bring with you the thoughts you carry and embed them in your body to awaken the cells, to connect the DNA constructs to clear the mitochondria and reconnect the RNA authentic to mother. Ask for the truth to shine brighter than self-doubt and ridicule.

I would like to add this; If every moment of doubt turns into defeat, the controllers win. I do not know who coined the term "whoever controls the mind controls the soul," but it is the single most profound statement I have read. Over and over again, I see friends, family, and clients not in control of their minds. They have unwittingly handed over their sovereignty to anyone/anything willing to "help." It is much like signing a contract without reading the fine print, and it says signer agrees to give up all original thoughts, health outcomes, a perspective of self, and the knowledge of the language of love.

How can we source the truth if our voice isn't our own?

Command it to be so by standing in your light and truth. When declaring your sovereignty for the world to know, your reality may recreate. Each memory has a timeline. Each timeline has a story. You have created thousands of millions of stories throughout your lifetime. Your thoughts grow like fruit on the trees, and yet you've put effortless thought into each of them. What happens when you claim sovereignty and choose your thoughts and emotions, thus creating a reality that suits you. It's a simple act. You just don't see it as such.

I have found in my learning/teachings that declaring sovereignty is one of the most critical and essential steps in healing. I would like to invite you to create your declaration. A pre-written declaration from someone else will do, or you may choose to create your own. There will be more power behind using your own words through your voice and conviction. Your truth is your truth, and no others. What matters is that you say it with certainty and belief and that you prepare to serve.

"My declaration of intention is to serve my highest god self. I intend to serve my highest self wholeheartedly, entirely, and completely. I Am God; I Am Sovereign, I Am Free."

When we show up to understand the deeper meaning of life, the truth behind humanity, and why it is we came here in the first place, we will never look into the eyes of another and see them as separate again. When we can see ourselves within everything around us, we are likely going to want to see and feel the love in every moment.

How can we know love in each moment?

When you were a little girl trying to figure out why everything already had a name, we were able to show you how to create your reality. Your thoughts were not predetermined by what those around you taught you; when time in your mind had passed, you were pre-conditioned to oblige society mandates. One cannot give a name to that which already has a name, but take away the label, and the thing or person or whatever just is.

The answer the Guides provided was a little confusing, as it was about a memory of mine. I will try to convey meaning. Compassionate witnessing begins with the clearing of the belief structures housed within our body-mind-spirit. Some of the most challenging healing I have done was through creating a new reality for the situations in my life that had happened. Once I had recognized that through love, we could change our perceptions, there was no stopping me from creating the life I wanted to live. The story I am about to share may trigger memories within your body-mind-spirit. Please proceed with caution.

Sexual trauma, addiction, and tyranny were top on my list of painful realities I came to this planet to help heal. When I was a little girl, age two, sexual abuse happened upon me. I remember the older man with weathered, wrinkled skin who always smelled of alcohol. I remembered a dark room with the scent of bodily fluids and the feeling of terror. I recall cold toilets and blood. I never remembered much of what happened as I would leave my body, so I didn't have to witness the trauma. I only remembered coming back and walking amongst a dirt back yard and chickens.

The abuse created splintering in my light body, which created pattering of violence to follow me through most of my life.

In 2007 I began my most significant Dark Night of the Soul that created a catalyst of events to heal the trauma within. When pain would arise in my body, I would stop and feel into that pain. Asking why you are here, what do you want? How can I help you?

You see, when we are not fully awake or in alignment with truth, fear arises spontaneously, which emits an energy frequency called loosh. When this happens, the negative energy is harvested and used for various nefarious purposes by the negative controller groups, otherwise known as the NAA or the cabal. The younger abuse can occur; the longer dark entities can siphon your energy and control your mind and direct your soul. The earlier the trauma, the stronger we unwittingly build the houses of ego. Once we have successfully constructed a strong ego base, we believe the abuse is caused by ourselves, thus created a lifetime of potential Satanic Ritual Abuse or SRA. Defined in the Ascension Glossary "SRA is a trauma-based method used to achieve the result of completely controlling the mind, to take complete control over people, and further abuse their bodies and souls." The usurped energy destroys our relationship and connection to God, Source, Universal-Realization, or whatever word you may identify as your higher sense of knowing.

To recreate your reality and live your life through the Christos eyes of love, you must tear down the old architecture. I share this short story with you because it was through witnessing the trauma and sending love in that moment of pain, that I was able to heal. Sending love does not equal condoning. It is equivalent to forgiveness. Forgiveness to the perpetrator and the self is needed to begin the healing. Ask your feelings and emotions what they need. Emotions will be stubborn, and thought-forms are hard to dissolve because you have been creating them all your life and the lives before that. Do not give up on yourself. Continue to ask with love, reach into your heart center and hold your inner self, the inner child, and say I Am Here Now. Forgive yourself for not being there in the darkest of times. For the deep-rooted emotions that rear their evil heads, command your sovereignty and with conviction, command that the thought-form entity dissolves and returns to Mother.

No matter how dark and daunting your journey may seem, look for the cracks where the light is shining. Lies cannot hold form in the light. For it is the truth that will set you free.

Go through every memory like this, and you will be able to tear down the old to build anew. I wish each of you many blessings on your healing journey.

JADEN FOX

JADEN FOX IS ONE of those fearless explorers who enjoys going where others dare not look. He's learned that our power and magic are being deliberately hidden from us by energies that are afraid of human's awakening and becoming conscious, and aims to change it.

His play is in empowering people to find themselves by clearing the illusions, distortions and limitation this reality has imposed while fostering expansive awareness of the true infinite magnitude of our authentic Being and Body. He's continually uncovering new ways to reconnect people to their power and magic so they can be the change they came here to be.

Jaden is an international presenter and facilitator of tools for awakening consciousness. He uses his wit, humor and authentic expression to awaken and inspire other way-showers to untangle limitation and connect to their inner clarity so they can step into what they came here to Be and do, NOW. He reconnects people to their Bodies, their potency and their playful magic while taking audiences beyond this matrix illusion and into their true magnitude beyond this universe!

Anyone ready to shed old patterns and viewpoints can be assured of going to expansive, fun and exciting places they have only imagined were possible.

How to find out more about Jaden Fox:

His website is https://www.jaden-fox.com/
Join https://www.facebook.com/JadenFoxCoaching
Contact him by phone at: +1(845) 202-9728

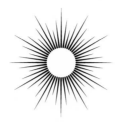

How to Evolve Beyond Alien Interference and Exit the Illusions of this Reality

BY JADEN FOX

Note:

In this chapter I will share things you have been programmed NOT to see.

Because of my being so direct, your old programming may trigger you to feel sleepy, blurry or a need to re-read this several times to hear the entire message.

If you are on a path of awareness or consciousness, you likely have invisible energies messing with you. They probably have been altering your reality for your entire life.

There are some people on this planet who recognize and accept the existence of aliens, entities and other non-physical beings, however, there are few who recognize these parasites could be actively be affecting their daily existence.

Some of you may think YOU are messing up your life because no matter how hard you try, life still sucks. But chances are, it's NOT you causing these problems.

Entities, angels/demonics, underworld creatures, aliens, gods and other non-physical beings that exist in the unseen layers of this world are also occupying this 3D Earth realm. These players are also involved in this world, altering things in a way that blocks awareness.

What if, as a being of the universe, you are in a relationship with all kinds of energies?

Some physical, some not. Some beneficial, some not. Some that hide and feed off you, some that don't.

Pretending you can't perceive these unseen energies doesn't mean that they don't interact with you.

It means that you aren't aware that they interact with you.

Do you ever have strange things occurring in your life? Odd unexplained glitches like a long string of negative experiences, or situations you know should unfold one way, but turn out the opposite.

Have you ever had the sense that something is messing with your life? If you have, you're right!

Signs You are Being Messed with:

The more unhappy you are, the more you are being influenced by external forces. Here are some common signs of interference:

- You feel you've lost yourself and can't get back
- You feel disconnected from your body or the planet
- You hear controlling voices in your head
- You keep getting stuck in a victim space or fear and can't get out

136

- You feel like your life has slipped backward, like nothing has ever cleared or changed
- You feel alien or that you don't belong in this world
- You get repeatedly triggered and feel unable to clear or remain aware
- You clear and clear, things keep coming back

etc…

If you are aware or conscious and things are not going as you expect, you are being actively messed with. But chances are it didn't just start. I suspect like other aware folks; you have been messed with your entire life.

From before you were born, invisible forces have altered your reality in subtle and harsh ways to steer you away from awareness. Interference has, instead, re-directed and conditioned you to make yourself wrong. Especially when you energetically bump into things you can't perceive or understand.

People who stay in the illusions and programming of this world and live as muggles, rarely experience direct interference because they are already controlled by mental programming. Once you learn to clear and break free from the programmed reality, the matrix takes a personal interest in you. Various agents of interference are sent your way to draw you back into the matrix, back into patterns of limitation. These active agents of interference are often the source of the odd things that occur in your life.

The further you bust out of limitation, the more advanced players show up and interact in your reality. The interference you experience becomes more dynamic and personalized. Interference messes with your thoughts and the people around you, intending to cause you to take actions that send you back into limitation.

Who is actually messing with your reality?

In the earlier stages of multi-dimensional awareness, you may find: angels/demons, arc angels, light beings, ghosts, underworld energies, and assorted non-physical creatures. Some are drawn to you by odd agreements you were tricked into. Others are directed towards you by agents of the matrix, usually as a distraction and entanglement.

If you are sensitive to ghosts (spirits of dead humans stuck in this reality) then the matrix of manipulators will keep magnetizing and dumping these energies in your reality, until you learn to identify them them and clear them.

It's like when you break free from one layer of limitation and constraint, a different set of players show up to tangle things in a new way. This seems to continue until you can recognize and work around their common games.

So in the earlier levels of awakening, you are baited or lured by beings pretending to want to help you, but who have a subversive agenda. They attempt to trick you into working with them and they promise you all kinds of things but in the end they just seek to tangle or use you. Their big goal at this level is to trick you into agreements and relations that are not what they seem to be.

As you increase your awareness and learn to bypass this previous layer of interference you find more sophisticated beings: a hierarchy of alien energies and lower level gods along with Synthetic Mind Systems (off-world AI) that begin showing up in your reality more.

These energies are more overtly controlling and more skilled at installing convincing illusions and stronger manipulations into your reality. These guys play in a deeper layer of mind manipulation. They love to insert thoughts into your mind and play with your polarized beliefs. They often seek to hide in your reality and trick you into thinking they are you. But they are not local to this planet they are distant and foreign, so with practice, you identify these energies and their games.

From one perspective these energies are determined to keep you unconscious and struggling. Yet, from another perspective, they provide additional challenges that invite you to expand your awareness and capacity and become stronger so you can out-create them and become more powerful.

As you increase your awareness and potency more and become effective at countering or eliminating the previous players, you find even more sophisticated beings start interacting with you: advanced aliens, higher-level gods, higher-level mind controllers and shape-shifting "slippery beings."

These players are more interactive yet very subtle. They look for any areas of unconsciousness you have and seek to hide in that and use it against you. Their primary game is to hide inside your body or reality and look for subtle ways to distract and influence you to not do what you came here to do. They are insidious, cunning, focused and harder to track, forcing you to become even MORE AWARE!

If you keep working to be consistently more aware and more powerful, you naturally expand into more of you, and fewer things can mess with you. You figure out their games and kick out the manipulators allowing you to take back your reality and body.

People often think, *"Why would any alien or god waste their time trying to stop me?"*...I'm just a pathetic, powerless, Earth human...But you're not!

You have been invited by the Prime Creator and likely even helped to design or create this universe on some level. You are also a creator sourced from beyond this realm, who has powerful connections and influence here in this universe.

The more you become aware of these invasive players the more you recognize that they are actually afraid of you.

They know your true power as a co-creator, they know you have the power to banish them from this reality and they want to prevent you from stepping into your power and awareness so they can preserve the corruption they have created here.

Many people assume they are afraid of aliens, gods, demons, but actually they are afraid of YOU!

Interference is afraid that you will:

- Learn the truth about who you are (and step into your potency & clarity)
- Discover the depth of interference behind your entire life (their cover will be blown)
- Get together with like-minded people and change this world (dismantle their fragile system)
- Get clarity about what's happening on this planet (and shut down their agenda)
- Feel good about yourself and step into your potency (removing them from your life)
- Create nurturing and supportive relationships & friendships (no longer feeling isolated & disconnected)

Interference is afraid because they are weak compared to you. You are naturally connected to an unlimited source of power and information. These corrupted energies have no such connection. They are parasites that have to scavenge to get what little energy they can. So they have evolved to be masters of deception, illusion and stealing energy!

The rules of this universe are such that THEY CANNOT OVERTLY CONTROL YOU. There is a degree of free will required here. But the rules do not prevent them from tricking you into systematically surrendering your free-will to them.

So the game they play is using highly organized illusions, mental games and tricky agreements to get you to limit and block yourself while surrendering your free will.

Most of this reality is NOT what it appears to be. It's a complex facade that tricks you into playing small, weak and unaware. It tricks you into not knowing the power and magic that you have.

Aliens and gods have no power to control you. But they are deeply skilled at using distortions and games to invite you to limit yourself and trick you into making yourself wrong and small.

Your Truth was Hidden from You

This reality has been systematically altered to obstruct awareness. It attempts to get you to be the opposite of who you truly are. It's an off-world agenda to hide your truth from you and discourage awareness.

See if you recognize the major strategies that interference commonly uses on humans:

- Interference has manipulated your childhood to have you feel deeply inferior, eliminate any self-esteem and encourage you to give your power & choice away to everyone else. Their goal is to have you not love or even like yourself, but to have you view yourself and your life as a total failure.

  + Reconnecting to your truth allows you to step into your self-confidence and embody the brilliance and skillfulness you truly are. You are naturally self-confident and skillfull.

- Interference wants you to be afraid of anything new or supernatural. They have conditioned your childhood to make you cautious, afraid to be curious and be afraid to explore outside of socially programmed norms.

  + Releasing your past allows you to go back to being: naturally bold, courageous redundant fearless and endlessly curious.

- Interference has done things to have you feel you don't belong in your family, society and this planet. They seek to isolate you from aware people like yourself and those who would inspire you to become more. They'll even insert programming to make you feel as though YOU are the alien here.

> + Clearing this programming allows you to FEEL a deep connection and sense of belonging to the natural world. From this space, you recognize the interference that does not fit in here. You are deeply connected to this Planet and Universe, and your presence is important here.

- Interference wants you to conform to the programmed reality, so you feel bored, uninspired, unimaginative and weary. The goal is to limit your self-expression so you feel stagnant, purposeless and unfulfilled. They want you to live a life feeling trapped in dead-end meaningless and ungratifying work and relationships.

> + Detaching from this programming opens the space to be inspired, creative and have meaning. Your natural state is to be deeply creative, involved, and inspired.

- Interference has worked to deeply distort this reality as to make it all very disorientating and so you feel you are going crazy. The message broadcast by interference is that you are weak and insignificant and that you should surrender to the program rather than be yourself.

> + Seeing through these illusions lets you be aware, be powerful and do what you most desire, to be your authentic self—however that shows up.

You are a naturally self-directed and powerful creator.

- Much of this reality is not what it appears to be. Interference has used hiding, deception, and distortions to alter this reality and your life, to prevent you from comprehending the big picture.

Where you have discovered the truth, they create disinformation to muddy the waters so the truth is hard to detect in the noise.

+ Being willing to see the truth of this reality lets you trust your authentic inner knowing and truth, your life and this world become clear and simpler to navigate. You are naturally connected to CLARITY & TRUTH.

Solutions:

Over the last 10 years, our team has been cataloguing the nature of interference on this planet and discovering how they mess with awakening humans. We've learned both how to stop them and how to teach the steps necessary to out-create and eliminate this interference for you and this planet.

Interference is only successful when you can't see their strategies and don't recognize their manipulations. When you see the impact interference has on your life and this reality, you'll naturally and automatically work around it.

Awareness is the key.

You really CAN eliminate or drastically reduce the amount of interference in your life, no matter how severe it seems.

In my past, my body and I have experienced being hopelessly and completely taken over by many different entities, gods, demons, aliens, creatures and countless unseen traps. But I found my way out, and you can too. Now I show others how to get out, so they can show others how to exit the limitations that exist here. My target is to see the entire planet awaken and get free. I'm here to change this reality.

I've just touched the surface of the games going on in this reality, but not shared how to change this.

In part 2, I'll share more solutions with you. The "how-to" become aware and get free from the limitations and traps that exist here.

Part 2 includes:

HOW TO ELIMINATE INTERFERENCE & EMBODY YOUR POTENCY, CLARITY & MAGIC

1. Expand your viewpoint to embody the Infinite YOU
2. Clear the 9 things that hide the Authentic You
3. Release the polarized viewpoints that block clarity & tangle you
4. Release the agreements and binds that keep you limited
5. Become aware and banish the players that act as interference
6. Step into and OWN your magic & potency
7. Reclaim, Own and Protect YOUR Body & Planet

I want YOU to get free, so you can use your unique gifts to help free other people!

This chapter continues on my website.

Go to: http://www.jaden-fox.com/chapter-part2

NICOLE THIBODEAU

NICOLE THIBODEAU IS AN Oracle of Divine Transmissions. As a Channeler and Mentor, she supports, guides and assists women and men in connecting with their inner healing gifts, and the achievement of clarity, peace, and understanding of themselves and their divine purpose on earth at this time. What Nicole is most passionate about is assisting women and men embrace their power and be the masters of their life.

She offers mentoring through her own programs, Unveil Your Inner Gifts™ & Embrace Your Divine Power™, in addition to soul healing sessions and channellings for groups.

In her channeled sessions, she uses light language and toning. She creates codes — images infused with high frequencies — to assist her clients to activate energies in a very simple, gentle and yet powerful way.

She works with clients from around the world and channels for groups in her community and internationally.

She lives in Canada.

How to find more about Nicole:

Her website is: https://nicolethibodeau.ca/
https://www.instagram.com/nicolethibodeau8/
https://www.facebook.com/nicolethibodeau.ca
Reach out to her by email@ info@nicolethibodeau.ca

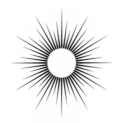

How to Embody Your Divine Self

BY NICOLE THIBODEAU

As a channel, I assist many people on their spiritual journey. I guide my clients carefully to ease the reconnection with their divine selves and to discover and develop their inner gifts. We are all a divine spark of God, of Source. Each person has innate inner gifts, which evolve with time and practice. You may already be aware of gifts like intuition, clairvoyance, clairaudience, or healing. When we make the choice to connect to our divine presence, we step into our power and become a divine human.

Most of us have that profound moment when we wonder and ask: "what if there is something bigger than me?" This question alone opens up the possibility to embark on a quest to discover your own truth. This new path enables you to open your heart to meaningful living and connection to your divine presence.

You can embody your divinity by bringing your divine energy into your daily life. Divine energies are the life force that live within your heart. They are the compassion, light, love and wisdom guiding us every day. You learn to live your divinity by inviting your divine self to guide you through your life.

You can embody your divinity with these simple steps:

- Close your eyes.
- Breathe deeply.
- Bring your attention to your heart center and heart chakra.
- Breathe into your heart to activate its sacred flame.
- Ground the sacred flame of your heart to the Earth and to Divine Source
- Gently, bring your attention back to your heart center.
- Sit in your heart center, breathing deeply and call to your Divine Presence to come.
- Connect your heart to your Divine Presence's heart.
- Allow the divine energy to flow freely through your heart.
- Receive from your Divine Presence.

Your trust will grow each time you connect to your divine self. Eventually unconditional love will pour through your heart into all areas of your life. You become love and open the connection to the higher frequency pathways and tap into greater potentials for you.

Your connection to your divine presence helps you have more clarity in your life. You will feel love filling your heart from the inside instead of trying to fill your heart with the love of others.

There are three major hurdles that could stop you from creating a deep connection to your divine presence. These three obstacles take the shape of thought-patterns, unconscious habits and belief systems. These can block or dim your divine connection and require healing to strengthen your divine connection.

How do thought-patterns impact the connection to your divine self and where do they come from?

Thought-patterns come from insults, unpleasantries and other negative things spoken to you as a child. Such comments root in your mind and bring you to think you are not worthy of divine connection. Negative belief systems, ingrained in the mind, make you believe that a divine connection is impossible because of your conclusions of unworthiness. Habits repeat themselves in different ways to support your erroneous beliefs and negative thought patterns. These three possibilities intertwine like a thick web that can initially prevent you connecting with your divine presence.

There are other negative beliefs that many adopt regarding the improbability of connecting with their Divinity: only advanced people can create such connection or, "I can't do this on my own, someone needs to hold the space for me." These thought-patterns, belief systems and fears can originate from this lifetime or from other lifetimes.

Your divinity is innate, and it requires acknowledgement so it can support you. Look inward and listen to your divine wisdom.

These four actions you can will help you feel centered, confident, and whole:

- Give yourself permission and time to connect to the divine within you
- Call in assistance from your guides.
- Trust that you are guided at all times and safe.
- Allow the divine wisdom to express through you.

In the first 20 some years of my life, I wasn't aware that I was highly intuitive. When I started experiencing premonitions, I didn't know what they were nor understood why I was experiencing them.

Sometimes the intuitions appeared as visions or experiencing what others felt. At other times, as an inner knowing, a deep feeling that something was about to happen. I used to say to my guide team that I was fine when they occurred, but the premonitions frightened me. I had so many questions and I had no one to turn to for answers. Many years went by before I understood why I had these visions and how they served me.

I thought everybody could sense or feel the same things I did. This wasn't the case. I even got angry sometimes, because people didn't see or feel what I could. Eventually, I understood that everyone is at different stages in their life journey, so what they heard or sensed would differ from what I did.

Do you ever feel disconnected, disorientated and fearful? In the early years of my awakening, I felt the same way. If you are judging yourself for having intuitions like I did, perhaps a part of you knows that something is knocking at your heart, desiring to be acknowledged and expressed.

Do you have persistent feelings that nudge you? And when you ignore or push them away, they just keep coming back stronger?

Often, we fight intuitions and premonitions because we fear them. I know I did. I felt worse and worse each time I denied my intuition; to a point where I began feeling tired and depressed. I even went to see a doctor and he couldn't find anything wrong with my health. I was still unhappy inside. I turned inward to find answers to heal myself.

You have the choice to work with your divine self or not. The importance of acknowledging your divine self is necessary for inner peace. Since it is part of who you truly are, it allows you to embrace all that you are.

Choice is something wonderful, even when difficult events occur in your life. You may not have chosen an event, but you can choose the attitude and the actions you will take facing these events. You have the choice to connect to your divinity and bring more peace in your life or not. You will feel happier and have more clarity when you live connected to your divine self every day.

What happens when you give yourself the time and space to reconnect within?

You anchor your heart flame to rebalance your energy, your chakra system and your bodies. When you sing from your heart, you re-harmonize yourself. As you connect to your divine presence, you receive its blessings. You have access to your divine wisdom to guide you each day. You receive the love and light needed to support you throughout your day and night. Each time you connect deeper to your divine power, the stronger you will feel from within.

Grounding your energy is as much your physical energy as your divine energy. It brings you strength and stability and helps you come back with ease into your own energy after a high frequency session. Grounding also helps you integrate the energies you received.

Not grounding may make you feel as if you were a thread floating in the wind of seemingly unstoppable events and conversations, unable to find your balance. To come back to a place of peace and balance: here is how you can center yourself and gain clarity.

- Sit quietly, where you can close your eyes for a moment.
- Take at least three deep breaths—Notice how your body feels
- Allow the thoughts to come and go
- Activate your heart flame
- Ground your heart flame to the earth's heart, also connecting your heart flame to Source Intelligence, which creates a beautiful pillar of light.
- Expand your pillar of light six feet in each direction, front, back and both sides as your pillar grounds to the earth's core.
- Breathe again in this space, you are safe.

- Receive the energies from the earth and Source and allow these energies to flow through you.

- You are now ready to continue your day or go into meditation. After your meditation, breathe deeply to come back fully in your body.

You can ground your energies as many times as you need each day. You must trust yourself: you will know when you require grounding for your well-being so you can feel balanced, connected and energized. You will feel so strongly grounded that negative events won't destabilize you as they did before. Your pillar of light protects you when your energies and your heart flame are anchored.

After you feel your energies anchored, invite your divine self to come to you. Together you will open your heart and connect to your divine wisdom. This wisdom lives within your heart and is always accessible when you're at peace. From this place, you can ask your divine presence all the questions you want.

Ask for guidance to learn about your inner gifts and to be shown how to best use them for your highest good and the highest good of all. We all have divine gifts to help and support us through our lives. These sacred gifts can be something we do regularly and naturally. Each time we do them, our hearts open and expand.

Which actions do you take that expand and fill your heart with great joy? Even little things as writing a simple note to wish a good day to a loved one or being present for others can fill your heart with happiness.

I was divinely guided to become a volunteer in a palliative care unit where I learned to work with an open heart. Each time before I entered the hospital; I would go into my heart, ask for divine inspiration to guide my words and actions. I didn't know the patients I would see, nor did I know their story, yet I offered love and compassion from my heart. Most times I followed the guidance of my divine self.

I remember one day hesitating to enter a patient's room. I felt this big nudge to go in, but my mind resisted and made me feel as if I was intruding on a very private moment. She was dying and her friend sat by her side. As my mind was questioning my intuition, her friend said, "please come in". She asked my name and then said to her dying friend: "isn't it lovely that she's coming to be with us now?" A few minutes later that patient passed away. Her friend confirmed my inner guidance. My presence in that room helped both the passing woman and her friend.

We all have examples of when we ignored our guidance. I remember the time I forgot to put my car pass on the dash of my car before my shift. Though I thought it would be ok, I ended up receiving a ticket. Staying connected to my divine presence helps me stay neutral or unaffected by difficult conversations or situations. I stay grounded and peaceful in my heart and body.

Allow your inner guidance to whisper to you through your heart and your actions. Sometimes you will receive confirmation. The more you pay attention to what is happening around you and how you feel, the better you understand how your divine guidance shows up for you. It also helps to make the difference between what belongs to you and what doesn't.

Check in to see if what you read, hear or perceive resonates with you. Then ask your divine presence if it is a truth for YOU. One's truth may not be so for you. Discernment is a major key in embodying your divine self.

Guidance drew me to two different spiritual schools. There, I connected to my divinity, through the Divine Mother's love. I learned to channel and do soul healing sessions. The teachings I received enable me to better help my clients in embracing who they are, bring peace to all facets of their being and embark on their spiritual journey.

Be patient with yourself. Do not compare yourself to others. You are unique and have your own distinct vibration. Expressing your divinity will resonate with your divine vibration. Each day, con-nect to your divine presence and open your heart to the highest potential for you. Trust your divine self, your guides and all the groups of divine light beings that are there to support you. Call them in to assist you as they await your call.

You are love.

You are light.

You are wisdom.

You are Divinity Embodied.

Linda Gifford

In the space of an instant, Linda's life was irrevocably changed due to a head-on car accident. As a result of her traumatic brain injury, Linda suffered memory loss and sustained multiple injuries throughout her body.

Using both Western medicine and Alternative modalities gave her the tools to recover. Her extensive research has led her to a compilation of a wide range of materials related to brain trauma.

Linda teaches others how to recover, restore and be at their best without the use of medications or surgery. She teaches these methods to others and inspires them to thrive.

Linda Gifford has taught health classes in doctor offices, as well as in the public sector. Including all ages of veteran's, people with traumatic brain injuries and post traumatic stress disorder, along with parents, children and caregivers who have brain related disorders.

In 2017 she was a featured speaker at the Northwest conference for Traumatic Brain Injuries which included the states of Alaska, Idaho, Washington and Oregon. Her growing list of students all started after 911 with firemen, police people, and traffic controllers working at a large international airport. Linda is working on her second book and currently resides in Portland, Oregon.

How to find out more about Linda:

Her website is: https://healbrainhealbody.com/

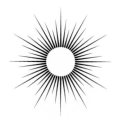

Prepare for Your First Class Flight

BY LINDA GIFFORD

THIS FLIGHT IS PREPARING for takeoff and leaving shortly. Please secure your attitude and blessings in a locked upright position. Please make sure all of your self-destructive devices are turned off. Put away all negative, hurt and discouragement.. Should you lose attitude under pressure during this flight please reach up and pulled down a prayer. Faith will automatically activate prayers. Once your faith activates, you can assist other passengers. There will be no baggage allowed on this flight. Now the captain has cleared us for takeoff! Hopefully, you have invited the ones you love and care for when you booked this First Class Flight, because our destination is a lifetime of love, joy and adventure.

Researchers around the world found that we first have a thought and then an emotion; before we have any ouch, illness, accident or disease. Repeatedly I ask my clients what they were thinking about and how did they feel, about that thought, an hour before they injured themselves or had to go to the emergency room because of a life-threatening health issue?

Money can't buy good physical or mental health. If you don't have good health, you can lose everything. You could lose your life savings, your retirement, your available credit, even your credit score. Your loved ones will stop wanting to be around you. You can lose the roof over your head, food, clothing, protection, a sense of self, your freedom, making your own decisions for yourself, your independence and so much more. I know this from personal experience.

One dark, rainy winter night, out of nowhere, a large Chevy spun out on the wet freeway pavement hitting me head on. The police report stated it was like my car hit a concrete wall going 185mph. When, in fact, I was travelling at a safe speed of 55 mph. In an instant, my life and my family's life changed forever.

Months and years went by, but the pain did not subside. My outside physical appearance began healing but my internal injuries and my brain did not. Both sides of my jaw fractured, my sinus cavity shattered, my tongue and lips wouldn't work when I tried to talk, form sentences or eat. My face, teeth, jaw, head and neck were screaming at a 10 plus pain level all the time. It was 18 months before they diagnosed me with a traumatic brain injury.

I had outbursts of anger, frustration and lengthy periods of wanting to do nothing except give up on life. Whenever life felt unbearable, I thought of a grandson who gave me special moments of joy. His curiosity and the magical moments we shared inspired me to learn more and to get better. He put laughter into my life when I had none. He delighted me as he taught me how to live through the eyes of an eight-year-old by mixing his joy with my despair and depression.

I had a conservator for 8 years who told me where to go, what to do and how to do it. I had no home, no car, and no way to earn a living. I lost most cognitive skills and my brain couldn't remember anything beyond three hours. The old me, a beautiful butterfly, disappeared, and I hid in a cocoon. I was inside my body, but very few people knew I was there.

Until the accident, I was a successful professional woman who took pride in my disciplined work. I went from dressing with style and earning a six-figure income, to requiring help with everything. Crying in frustration and bursting out in anger became the norm. Life stopped short, and I became frozen with grief and helplessness.

How does anyone recover from such devastating circumstances?

Beginning with the basics.

Look at the spokes of a bicycle tire rim. Every spoke must be the same strength to hold its shape when riding. It must be perfectly balanced all the way around for the best use and give the most joy from that wheel when riding. Each spoke represents our finances, spouse, kids, home, community and other joys in life. Just like the flight attendant tells to put your oxygen mask on first before you before you help other passengers.

Our cellular memory can heal like our thought memory can. Our cells regenerate continuously throughout our life. If this is the case, you might wonder, why do we age and fall apart? It's because our cells have memory. Our cells have a specific job. For instance, a cell in your little left finger is only responsible for that left little finger. When you are born, the first cell of the left little finger has an experience which records as a cellular memory on how to survive. Each cell, as it dies, passes along the information as stored cellular memory to subsequent replacement cells, all the way through your life. Look at people's fingers as they age. The true purpose of the cell in your left little finger is to do its job and survive until the next cell comes along as a replacement. A man who receives an organ transplant craves a particular hamburger he never had a hankering for before. He discovers the organ donor had a great love for eating those hamburgers.

Even though we feel we lost all control of our life and there's nowhere to go, it's important to remember sometimes we have to go back to the basics. Like, putting joy in our life wherever we can.

When people hurt physically, emotionally or mentally they do not make appropriate decisions for themselves or their loved ones.

Scientists have found our brain cannot function optimally if we are under stress or in survival.

You need not worry about viruses or bacteria if a tiger is about to eat you. You must escape the tiger first. You need not digest the food you eat if you are trying to avoid a bus coming right at you. Short-term memory is useless if a tiger is about to eat you. Sexual function is a mute issue if you cannot pay the rent or feed your family. Survive the stressful situation first before any of your physiological systems function optimally.

Logical thinking is too slow. You don't ponder the possibility that an old tiger looks like he has no teeth. Instead, you know you BETTER RUN.

What does this have to do with your day-to-day life? EVERYTHING!

The consequences of our thoughts and emotions improve our health. Our brain is like the hard drive on our computer. The programs are our digestive system, blood circulation, walking, talking and our thoughts, etc. A Window 7 computer can't run any of the programs from a Windows 10 computer hard drive.

Everything you do builds your First Class Flight. (LIFE CHOICES = First Class Flight). You can't expect others to make all of your life choices because you are the only one with your body 24/7. You must help yourself.

You must do a little every day. Every day work on your brain and body to keep it as healthy as possible.

Here are some specifics on how to Prepare for First Class Flight.

Most people think all they have to do is exercise and go on a diet. I recommend appropriate exercise along with a good organic, balanced diet. But there is more to balancing the brain and the body for optimal health.

To achieve the best outcome, choose only three techniques to start with. After you write them down, close your eyes, feel and picture your outcome successfully completed. After a month you can add three more changes to your daily routine.

Forgive yourself first and then others. Get specific on who you are forgiving and why.

Each day write five things that you are grateful for. Share these with others.

Make a joy bank. It can be a bowl, or a jar. Deposit three joyful things that you experienced each day. A joy bank is much like a savings account so when life hits you with unexpected disappointments, read a few JOYS to lift you out of despair.

Write 10 successes or accomplishments in life. These will pull you out of the whirlpool of self destruction or despair.

Get up every half hour and move. Stretch all of your muscles from your toes, legs, hips, waist, arms and neck.

Walk briskly for 20 minutes. A British study shows doing this you could cut dementia and Alzheimer's disease in half.

Sleep 7 to 8 hours a night with at least four hours continuously to get REM sleep.

Drink enough water slowly throughout the day.

Give anonymously from your heart each day.

Pray or meditate for 20 minutes a day.

Use all of your senses to connect deeply with nature each day.

Connect with people every day. It may be somebody while standing in line or a phone call to a wonderful friend. Texts, emails, twitters and Facebook etc. will not work. The brain and body require people contact to stay balanced. Balance and harmony ensure health and well being.

Give up judgments.

Learn something new each day. This creates new neurological pathways in your brain.

Be vulnerable and ask for help.

Listen to others with an open heart. It opens you to feeling resilient, resourceful, peaceful and empowered.

Believe in love when it comes, it's all around us every day. If you believe in love when it comes in, healing happens. It's not how love is given, but how we process and accept love.

Go back to the basics. Put joy into your life wherever you can. Give to others especially when you're down. Look around at what you're grateful for. Create wholeness and well-being, not perfection. Look for the good that comes out of that experience. Thank others for being in your life by giving them examples of what they mean to you.

As we connect our brain with our body, we restore, remodel and repair our health. When our brain and body work at their best, our entire life works better for ourselves, our family and our community.

Stacy Gleich

Stacy Gleich resonates as an Enlightened Being. She is a Planetary and Akashic Healer.

Stacy and her husband Darryl currently reside in Maryborough, Queensland, Australia. Stacy specializes in physical, metaphysical, and emotional healing. Her forte is trauma removal and past life healing. Stacy is here to lift the vibrational level of awakening souls and to heal those that seek her energy.

She loves to dance.

How to find out more about Stacy Gleich:

Her website is: www.energy4living.com.au
www.instagram.com/energy4living
www.facebook.com/energy4living

Enlightened Awakening:
How to Consciously Recall Your Soul Divinity

BY STACY GLEICH

Discovering one's true purpose begins with aligning yourself to universal energies, and the centre of the cosmos. Love is the frequency that emanates from the heart of the Universe.

Remembering past incarnations of the beautiful souls you are should not unleash fear but excitement about the journey ahead. A paradigm of new and cosmic possibilities awaits the courageous. The many paths and lifetimes you have experienced prior to your current incarnation on Earth are a testament to your resilience.

Remembrance of your Akash can bring about life- altering scenarios to explore. Akashic records are a timeless library, an energetic blueprint of all the lifetimes you have lived. These records offer a chronology of your highest development in an ever expanding infinite universe. They hold your energy purpose in a non-physical realm. There are professional Akashic record readers, or you may find as you attain higher consciousness that your Akash will reveal itself in universal divine timing. These multidimensional records can show up through dreams, thoughts and sudden revelations.

Through meditation you can move to a higher vibration and consciousness. It is a place where you connect to your higher self. While meditation offers many discoveries, the following exercise enables you to attain higher consciousness by expanding the power of your pineal gland.

Find a quiet and peaceful place, with no interruptions. Be comfortable either sitting or lying down. Close your eyes, relax all but your hands, through controlled breathing, in and out. Clench the hands tightly for 5 seconds, feel the tenseness release and allow yourself to relax completely. For this exercise we are going into the pineal gland. Your Third Eye surrounds your pineal gland and is found in the centre of your forehead, between your eyebrows. When you perceive your pineal gland gently open an imaginary door to go in. Once you have entered, look around. Is your pineal gland large or small? Imagine a golden light entering through the third eye, filling up the pineal gland. The golden light expands the pineal gland, making it infinite. After a few minutes notice what has changed. Acknowledge the changes, thank the universe and gently come back to the present.

Regular practice of this exercise will open a bridge to your intuition.

As you awaken, your intuition and inner guidance become stronger, like a dream trance you have awakened from. Your knowing becomes a powerful indicator of what is right for you. Second-guessing will no longer play such a strong role in your existence.

Real awakening begins when you have the courage to be vulnerable at your soul level. There is a place inside you that houses your soul, a level of self–awareness and thankfulness for being alive.

Many people discover unhealed trauma from this life and past lives. This holds them back from evolving.

Trauma is the darkness that shadows the light. It is the unnamed monster that dwells from the past with savage power.

Trauma becomes the accumulation of events you stored in your energy field from all lifetimes. It locks in the energy at the original point the trauma occurred. To clear it, you need to go back to the event and change the energy around the trauma before it releases its power over you. After that, trauma transforms into a distant memory that no longer bothers you. It no longer makes you feel tense, angry, unloved, unwanted or stressed. When trauma heals, it lightens your energies. The best version of you appears in perfect soul alignment. For some clients:

The mirror reflects an unworthy image,
Distorted in the lies it tells,
If only you could see what I can see,
The truth of your beautiful soul.

Some individuals require authentic healers to clear held trauma. Most are not aware that the traumas they experienced in this lifetime activate past life traumas with similar themes of abuse, rejection and fear.

I worked with a client who suffered abuse in her relationship. This mirrored what happened to her in 2 previous lifetimes—one in the 8th century, and the other one in the 17th century. It was possible for me to time line back to with her to heal her wounds from these previous centuries, before returning her to her current life and the point at which her abuse had occurred, and completing her healing.

Allow the universe to guide you in its wisdom about what is right for you. In that space, you will discover answers to your inner calling.

When you energetically commit to the path of the universe, your soul is empowered to undertake a journey of enlightenment. Do not allow negative emotions to overtake you or surround you with fear.

Fear is a response to the unknown; enlightenment and wisdom is the light to overcome it. You will get to a point in your own evolution when you can no longer ignore the questions you have about your life purpose and spiritual mission.

To assist with your evolution, allow your heart to open and connect to the energy of Love, the highest frequency within the Universe. The heart is an expansion of pure emotion, a deep well of beautiful unconditional love. Your Heart is the centre of All That Is. It is time to honor the journey your heart has taken; it is an energetic dynamo of feelings and energy. Splintered and wounded over time, your heart typically holds pain from multiple lifetimes.

Find a place that is peaceful and serene, breathe deeply in and out and journey deep into your heart. Imagine a silver thread weaving through your heart creating positivity and loving kindness. Become still, as if time itself had stopped. Immerse yourself in the moment's beauty. Then allow the feelings to flow from your heart to all that you are. Gently open your eyes and come back to the present when you are ready.

Express gratitude for receiving such a precious gift of Self Love. Gratitude is the calling card of the Universe and the gateway of appreciation for all that we have and all that we are. To live in gratitude is to give thanks on an energetic level. This vibrates through the collective and assists those ready for transformation. The collective is all the souls on planet Earth; each one on their own journey of discovery.

There is a monumental shift in consciousness happening on earth now, and we are all a part of the process. Perhaps you may recognise energies of higher consciousness appearing in your daily life. Feelings of peace, and heart-felt kindness offered to those in need all help to move humanity forward in a positive and uplifting way. Individuals uniting in times of tragedy and disasters also help to strengthen humanity's higher energies. Unlike any other time in history many of us are joining as One to assist, and care for others.

The veils of duality and illusion are dissipating. The fog of amnesia is lifting from souls who forgot their infinite nature and are now beginning to remember who they truly are.

Together we hold and shine the light on untruths and falsehoods that governed this planet for centuries and bound its citizens by mind control, fear, and conditioned enslavement at the hands of a powerful few.

The dark controllers have paved a road that leads to and through destruction and pain. Greed, hate and ego create ever darker depths.

Now humanity awakens and steps into its power; rejecting fear-based beliefs and rising like a Phoenix out of the fire. The old energy of darkness is being forced out, and the matrix of control is being forever destroyed.

Judgment is the failing of the human mind, a narrow thought process not yet touched by higher consciousness. The lower vibration of the old energy is no longer in play and is now replaced by Cosmic Consciousness, a higher vibrational energy, awakening souls and lifting humanity out of the darkness. It is calling upon us to be authentic and to stand in the truth of who we are, stripped of our human ego, healed from our pain and trauma; transformed into beacons of light to show the way forward. The truth is that internal fulfillment can be found within every one of us.

New Energy brings ascension, a process of enlightened awakening and expanded consciousness through cosmic energetic upgrades rising to a new level of being.

Galactic realms are forever changing and showering humanity with high-powered, photon light energy for accelerated change. High vibrational energy is bringing forth truth and understanding of who you truly are.

Lightworkers and Star Seeds are waking up to be part of the light collective. Lightworkers are connected to interdimensional energies around the earth. Since their origin is slightly above third-dimensional frequencies, they are very connected to earth. Their purpose is to raise the vibration of the planet. Highly evolved Star Seeds from distant planets, galaxies, dimensions and parallel universes, are here to birth and support a new consciousness.

Ascension is moving to a lighter state of being in connection with releasing all programmed beliefs of the old energy. This process can be difficult and uncomfortable at times.

When solar storms appear and portals are opened, activations and energy shifts manifest as physical and emotional stress. Feelings of confusion and not understanding what is happening occur, as well as nausea, headaches, body pain, tiredness, and feeling disconnected from the third dimension can result in a feeling of being out of balance. We are all energetic beings inhabiting a human form.

Grounding yourself to the earth during these high vibrational shifts is beneficial. Start with the heart, as the energy is always the highest there. Breathe slowly and deeply with purpose, and imagine the heart becoming still and centred. See the energy moving through your chakras starting with the crown and moving down through the third eye, throat, heart, solar plexus, sacral and root chakra. Allow the energy to continue downward through your feet until you see roots going deep in the Earth.

Himalayan salt baths may also assist you in creating mental, spiritual and emotional balance. Connecting with like-minded souls going through the ascension process brings about greater understanding.

When you are ready, the teacher will appear, and this will help you to open the window of consciousness. A mentor who can guide you through the invisible universe that is not seen by the eye but felt by the heart, can assist you in moving through energetic gateways of vibration and energy.

Cosmic coincidences are meaningful synchronicities that will lead you to events, people and information that you never knew about.

The universe, through its own deeper intelligence, will attract to you people you are meant to meet and situations that will stretch your awakening and enlighten your journey.

When you remove doubt and fear by allowing inner trust, you allow the Universe to guide you. Higher Self Guidance leads you to the things required for your soul growth. This is always cosmically ordered from the highest source, the Eternal Universal Creator. This Source intelligence is always operating on a deeper level; sometimes you will know it. This will always be for your highest good. The path to enlightenment is yours and yours alone. No two journeys will be the same.

The storm of life will never cease,
It blows its torrent with undue ease,
Sweeping through in all seasons,
There is no path or given reason,
Given to us to cherish every meeting,
How we use this gift,
A waste of time is always that,
A choice we make, a chance gone by,
A consequence to live and sometimes die,
The seasons turn and as they do,
Life transitions through the answers we never knew.

Journey well my friends.

CONCLUSION

Have we touched the Infinite Being deep inside you, awakening you to a different reality? Have we inspired and guided you to heal more of you so that you can remember your union with the Creator of All? Are you now ready to shed your small self and your ego and align with the Infinite Greatness you be?

Who would have thought that Infinite Beings birthed from the divine union of an omnipotent feminine and masculine Source of creative intelligence would have forgotten.......the power they had to create new worlds?

Never before in the history of humanity, has our awakening been necessary to the survival of our species and Mother Earth. We can not heal humanity until we heal ourselves. Choosing to become conscious is a revolutionary act. Your choice to heal is an evolutionary act.

What would it take for you to let go of all the lies of you and the lies of this reality and reclaim your infinite nature as the One Love Consciousness that you are? What if that alone could lift humanity and Earth into a new reality?

Because we are Creator Beings, the choices we make and what we align our energies with, will create new realities. What we choose to embody affects the entire human race. Are you willing to know who you are in the truth that you are? To look at your Self in a new light and claim your God, Sovereign, Free being, the real you, in order to create and embody a new reality on Earth?

Now is the time. What will you choose?

SOVEREIGN · FREE · GOD ·

Made in United States
North Haven, CT
19 April 2022

18388751R00109